AN INTRODUCTION TO MICROCOMPUTERS

Volume 0
The Beginner's Book
Third Edition

AN INTRODUCTION TO MICROCOMPUTERS

Volume 0
The Beginner's Book
Third Edition

Adam Osborne
David Bunnell

Published by
OSBORNE/McGraw-Hill
630 Bancroft Way
Berkeley, California 94710
U.S.A.

For information on translations and book distributors outside of the
U.S.A., please write OSBORNE/McGraw-Hill at the above address.

AN INTRODUCTION TO MICROCOMPUTERS: VOLUME 0
THE BEGINNER'S BOOK THIRD EDITION

34567890 DODO 8976543

ISBN 0-931988-64-0

Cover design by Lorli Willis

Trademark
Acknowledgments

The italicized names are trademarks of the following companies with registered trademarks noted with®:

alphaSyntauri® Syntauri Corporation

ATARI® *400/800*® *Computer* Atari, Inc.

Apple® *II, Apple*® *III, Graphics Tablet*® Apple Computer, Inc.

CBM, CBM 2001, CBM 8000 series, PET®, *PET*® *2001, VIC* Commodore Business Machines Inc.

CP/M® Digital Research®

IBM® IBM

Osborne 1 Osborne Computer Corporation

Panasonic® Panasonic

SAM, 820 Xerox Corporation

Softcard, Typing Tutor Microsoft Inc.

The Source (Servicemark) Source Telecomputing Corporation

SuperCalc Sorcim

System X-10® BSR (USA) Ltd.

T/Maker P.Roizen

TRS-80® *Model II, TRS-80*® *Model III,* Tandy Corporation

UCSD Pascal Regents of the University of California

WordStar MicroPro International Corporation

VisiCalc® VisiCorp

Z80® Zilog, Inc.

Contents

Introduction

Microcomputers are destined to be ranked alongside automobiles and television sets as among the most significant inventions of the twentieth century.* By now you've probably seen a microcomputer — perhaps in your local electronics store — and you know about the tiny silicon chips that have made microcomputers possible. What you may not realize is that **within the next few years microcomputers will be as common in our everyday lives as the telephone.**

If you know little or nothing about computers of any kind, this book will get you started, whether you want to buy your own computer, or learn how computers work and how they are built. Accordingly, the book is divided into two sections of three chapters each. Section I (Chapters 1-3) examines the features of microcomputers and related products such as printers and disk drives in enough detail that if you should decide to buy your own system, you can avoid most of the common pitfalls. You will also learn what microcomputers do and how they do it. Section II (Chapters 4-6) is for those readers who want to learn about the inner workings of microcomputers and the

---

* The text of this book has been printed in **boldface** and lightface types in order to let you bypass information you already know and dwell on information you do not yet understand. **Boldface text summarizes all major subject matter.** When you come across anything in boldface you don't understand, then read the accompanying lightface text for extra information.

technical principles upon which they function. Should you study the second half of the book and find yourself eager for still more information, you may want to move on to the next book in this series, *An Introduction to Microcomputers: Volume 1 — Basic Concepts.*

Do you have to understand the internal workings of microcomputers in order to use them? Not really. If people had to understand how automobiles work in order to drive, the number of automobiles on the road would be substantially reduced.

However, while automobiles benefit from nearly 100 years of engineering refinement, microcomputers are relatively new. Just as early automobiles had their quirks, such as hand cranks, today's microcomputers are much less accessible to the average person than models that are still on the drawing board.

Compared with the current crop — the Xerox SAMs, Apples, IBM personal computers, and Radio Shack TRS-80s — the first microcomputers were really tin lizzies. You couldn't go down to a computer or electronics store and buy one; you had to order your microcomputer through the mail. Furthermore, you couldn't just plug it in. You had to build the computer from a kit, which included such parts as transistors, chips, diodes, circuit boards, wires, and, if you were lucky, a reasonably accurate instruction manual. Building a microcomputer required a soldering iron, a pair of needle-nosed pliers, and a great deal of patience. And once you built your microcomputer, there wasn't much you could do with it other than program its front panel lights to blink on and off in predetermined patterns. To make your microcomputer useful required additional interface and memory boards that plugged into the microcomputer's "bus." Once you built these "options," you could connect your microcomputer to peripherals such as teletype machines, computer terminals, and line printers. What began as a $400 kit often turned into a $10,000 "system" — and even then, you had to do most of the programming yourself, since few programs were then on the market.

The early microcomputer users were commonly known as "computer hobbyists." Many of them were engineers or programmers who built computers in their spare time. Their fascination with computers was such that they really didn't mind the fact that their microcomputers, once built, were virtually useless.

The first generally available microcomputer kit to appear on the scene was the Altair 8800, featured on the January 1975 cover of *Popular Electronics* magazine. It was the brainchild of a retired Air Force engineer, Ed Roberts, who owned a tiny company named MITS in Albuquerque, New Mexico.

Some of the early microcomputer owners used their expertise to develop products that propelled the microcomputer from the hobbyist market to the consumer, electronic, and small business markets.

Microdome's "two Steves" — Stephen Wozniak and Steven Jobs — were directly responsible for making microcomputers more accessible when they designed the first Apple computer in Jobs' parents' garage. The Apple I was one of the first microcomputers to combine important components such as memory, intelligence, input, and output on a single circuit board. Its enthusiastic reception at the Homebrew Computer Club, a hobbyist club in the San Francisco Bay Area where Wozniak and Jobs were introduced, convinced the two to upgrade the Apple I to the Apple II and to enter the microcomputer business. The result was Apple Computer Inc., which has become one of the most successful microcomputer companies, with revenues in excess of $100 million per year.

The Apple II and its competitors, the Commodore PET and the Radio Shack TRS-80, were much easier to use than the Altair 8800. These machines came with typewriter-style keyboards and video displays which replaced the rows of lights and toggle switches on the earlier hobbyist models. They also came with the BASIC computer language built in; you could use it the instant you turned on the machine. To use BASIC on an Altair you first had to set toggle switches on the front panel and load BASIC into the computer's memory from a paper tape reader (many early microcomputers were interfaced to surplus teletype machines). The whole process of simply getting to BASIC took 20 minutes to an hour.

The early microcomputer business faced a dilemma not unlike that which confronted the early hi-fi industry. People who purchased the first home hi-fi sets had problems locating an ample supply of records. Music companies were reluctant to invest large amounts of money in records until there were enough potential customers who owned record players. The incentive to buy hi-fi sets was in turn diminished because there weren't enough records on the market.

Microcomputers avoided this initial hurdle much sooner than did hi-fi because they are programmable. In effect, with a microcomputer, you can make your own "music."

Today there are literally **hundreds of companies that develop and distribute programs for microcomputers.** (Programs are generally termed *software*.) Many of these companies were started by computer hobbyists who, once they programmed their microcomputers to do something useful, decided to sell their programs to other users.

Thanks to these programmer pioneers, **you can make extensive use**

of a microcomputer simply by turning it on and loading a program. For example, **with software such as WordStar you can turn your microcomputer into a word processor** that lets you edit documents, letters, books, or manuscripts on the video display. When you have finished your editing, you press a few keys and the document prints in its final, edited form.

Many of the currently available programs for microcomputers are in the area of education. Microsoft, a company that produced the first microcomputer BASIC, sells a program called Typing Tutor that turns a microcomputer into an effective typing teacher.

One of the most successful microcomputer software products is VisiCalc, distributed by VisiCorp. Available for the TRS-80, Apple, Atari, and IBM personal computers, **this software turns the screen of your microcomputer into a sophisticated analytical tool, an *electronic spread sheet*** which has an unlimited number of rows and columns. At each row or column you can enter numbers, formulas for calculating the results of numbers, or descriptive labels for the data you entered. By changing other values, your data will be automatically recalculated. Thus, **VisiCalc is used by many business professionals as a tool for developing business and marketing strategies**.

Another way to use your microcomputer is to hook up to a computer network. This requires a device that lets you connect your microcomputer to a telephone. By dialing a phone number (a local call in most areas) your microcomputer connects to a central computer, a large "mainframe" machine. The network asks you for your account number and your secret code before it lets you proceed further. Once you are properly connected, you can access any number of services. For example, The Source network carries United Press International newswire stories which you can read on your screen. Most networks have games you can play and a message service which lets you instantly send and receive electronic mail from any of the other network customers, no matter where they might be located.

A complete discussion of all the programs and network services available for microcomputers would require a separate book. Still, **there are plenty of reasons for many users — perhaps, a majority — to learn how to program their own microcomputers.** As vast as the current collection of prepackaged programs is, it touches only a fraction of the microcomputer's potential. **One of the reasons microcomputers are bound to profoundly influence all aspects of society is that their uses are limited only by the creativity of the people who can program them.** The ability to program allows you to individualize your microcomputer to work exactly as you wish it to work.

To program a microcomputer, you need to learn a *programming language.* In a sense, you teach yourself to communicate with a microcomputer in much the same way that you might teach yourself to communicate with a person from a different country. Many programming languages aren't too difficult because they consist of English words.

The **most popular programming language used on today's microcomputers is BASIC.** This language was created by two Dartmouth professors, John Kemeny and Tom Kurtz, in 1964. Its purpose was to make computers more accessible to students. They accomplished this by making the language "interactive" and by using standard English code words. Interactive means that the computer responds directly and immediately to the input of the user. "Talking" to a computer then becomes similar to talking to a person.

Prior to BASIC, the most common method of programming was done with a process called batch FORTRAN. This was a slow and laborious method. Programs were first punched out on cards which were fed to the computer in one batch. The programmers would often have to come back the next day to see if the program worked correctly. Dartmouth's BASIC was an instant success, and soon it was duplicated on many different computers. Bill Gates and Paul Allen, the founders of Microsoft, implemented BASIC on microcomputers when they created Altair BASIC in 1975. Without their efforts, microcomputers would not have gained in popularity as rapidly as they did. Microsoft BASIC is available on many different microcomputers, and estimates are that more than half a million copies have been sold.

Other programming languages, such as Pascal and FORTH, are popular with microcomputer users. **Many programs are written with assemblers which, although less eloquent and more difficult to learn than so-called "higher language" programs, take full advantage of the microcomputer's capability and require much less memory space.** WordStar and VisiCalc were written with assemblers. A thorough explanation of programming and programming languages can be found in Chapter 3.

There is considerable debate in academic circles about **"computer literacy."** What is meant is that **people need to learn more about how computers work in order to take full advantage of them and to prevent others from abusing them.** But, while **one school of thought advocates "computer literacy," another advocates that computers be taught "people literacy."** This second school is saying that computers should be built to fit in with existing ways that people do things. People shouldn't have to understand so much about computers in order to use them. Computers should instead be made to understand people.

Notice that in this discussion of literacy we have used the word "computer" instead of "microcomputer." Is there any difference between these?

A microcomputer's size is not standard. It can be small enough to hold in your hand or as large as a desk top. The computer's logic is contained on a single microprocessor chip which we will describe shortly. **A microcomputer functions in the same way as a large computer.**

Large computers, which may vary from cabinet-sized minicomputers to room-sized "mainframe" computers, are more powerful than microcomputers — they **can process larger amounts of numbers or data in a shorter time**. Handling all the reservations for a major airline company requires a large computer. Microcomputers can do similar tasks, such as maintaining the schedule of a business executive, but only on a much smaller scale.

Because microcomputers are cheaper than other, larger computers, they can be used for many applications that previously weren't considered practical for computers. As a consequence, **the impact of microcomputers will be to expand the number of jobs that can be computerized**. Like microcomputers, big "mainframe" computers can store recipe files and play computer games, but they are best used performing "cost-effective" tasks.

Everyone is aware that computers have already had a big impact on society. **During any normal day, your life will be touched by computers many times.**

For instance, your name is probably on mailing lists maintained by computers. A large computer can print thousands of address labels in a minute. If typists had to type address labels, you would receive less mail; the senders could simply not afford the cost of the typists.

Credit cards exist because of computers. If accountants did all of the bookkeeping associated with credit card accounts, the cost of accounting would make credit cards uneconomical.

Consider a previous example — airline ticket reservations. You can walk up to a ticket counter and request a reservation on any flight, anywhere in the country. The ticket agent is able to tell you instantly whether seats are available; if you make a reservation, it is recorded instantly. If another customer, hundreds of miles away, requests the same seat ten seconds later, the customer will not be sold your ticket. Overbooking may occur, but computers tell the airlines exactly how many tickets have been sold, and on which flights.

In 1950 there was just one commercially available computer — the ENIAC 1. Originally developed to handle the U.S. Census, this computer filled up a large room, required special air conditioning, and cost more than $500,000 (that is, 1950 dollars).

Not realizing that less expensive computers could be utilized for a multitude of tasks, some scientists at the time thought a dozen or so "supercomputers" should be built to handle all the data processing needs of the United States. Fortunately the scientists were wrong. In 30 years, the **cost of computing power equivalent to the ENIAC 1 has dropped to less than $10 (1981 dollars).** In the late 1950s and early 1960s, computers costing $1 million or more started to handle data processing for very large companies, those who could afford the high price. Today an equivalent computer system is available for $2000 to $3000 — cheap enough to do the bookkeeping for the local drugstore.

The most significant development in the first 30 years of computers was the invention of the microprocessor — popularly known as the "computer on a chip." First introduced by Intel Corporation in 1972 as the result of a research project headed by E. M. Huff, the **microprocessor compacts the equivalent of more than 10,000 electronic components (transistors, diodes, and so on) on a chip of silicon about the size of a cornflake. These components, which once filled dozens of circuit boards, are the ones that make up the logic of a computer.**

The technology for jamming an ever increasing number of components into a single package — known as large-scale circuit integration — can be traced further back to the space programs of the 1960s. In order to hurl men out of the earth's atmosphere in sophisticated rocket ships, it was necessary to develop ways to compress electronic components into small, lightweight packages.

But once the United States reached its goal of sending astronauts to the moon and returning them safely, the nation's interest in the further development of space technology declined rapidly. This left thousands of engineers with no jobs and nothing to do except start commercial enterprises based on the new technology they learned while working for the government.

These engineers-turned-entrepreneurs were responsible for creating the huge semiconductor industry centered primarily in Northern California's "Silicon Valley" about 50 miles south of San Francisco. Silicon Valley is the home of Intel, Hewlett-Packard, Apple, and many other high-tech companies.

The microprocessor led the way for the microcomputer. However, while the brains of the computer are being compacted into integrated circuit chips, other components such as memory and interface logic (the part that lets you connect to other devices) are also being compacted onto chips. When the Altair was introduced in 1975, its memory chips could each contain 1000 bytes or units of information. Today's memory chips contain as many as 65,000 bytes and there is no end in sight. (A *byte* is a unit of memory roughly capable of storing one character, a letter of the alphabet, or one digit of a number.)

At the time of this writing, there were approximately 500,000 working microcomputers. By the time you read this book there will be significantly more. New microcomputers are being announced weekly, and new microcomputer programs come out daily. Major computer companies such as IBM, Xerox, and Hewlett-Packard have moved into a market that was once the exclusive domain of companies like Apple and Cromemco. Meanwhile, Japanese electronic giants including Fujitsu, Hitashi, and NEC are poised for major moves into the U.S. microcomputer marketplace.

Where it will all end is anybody's guess. The Osborne 1 microcomputer, which folds up into a briefcase, may be the forerunner of book-sized microcomputers which we will carry with us almost everywhere we go. Already there are small microcomputers with limited capacity, including the Radio Shack Pocket Computer. The April 1981 cover of *BYTE* magazine showed a possible future microcomputer wristwatch, complete with a full typewriter keyboard and thumbnail-sized floppy disks.

What we do know is that there is a microcomputer in nearly everyone's future. The time to start learning about microcomputers is now. We hope you find this book to be an informative and entertaining beginning.

1
The Parts That
Make the Whole

In the Introduction, we defined a **microcomputer as a handheld or desk-top computer with its** *brains*, **or logic power, contained on a single microprocessor chip.**

At present, there are **hundreds of microcomputers on the market** in a multitude of shapes, sizes, and colors. The Sinclair ZX80, the Radio Shack Pocket Computer, the Apple II, and the Osborne 1, as shown in Figure 1-1, are all microcomputers.

Microprocessor Chip

As you might surmise from Figure 1-1, **the microprocessor chip is often the only common item between two microcomputers. But the microprocessor chip may also be the only distinction between a small computer and a large computer.**

ENIAC, the first computer, had 19,000 vacuum tubes — instead of a single microprocessor chip — to handle its computing function. Keeping ENIAC running required a whole team of technicians whose sole function was to find and replace faulty tubes.

Semiconductors

Vacuum tubes were replaced in the 1950s by smaller, more reliable devices called transistors. **Transistors are made of solid state materials called** *semiconductors* **through which the desired level of electric current can pass.** The development of transistors gave way to much more powerful, cheaper, and smaller computers. The average size of a computer shrank from room-sized to refrigerator-sized.

Large Scale Integration

The brains of these second-generation computers consisted of about a dozen circuit boards "stuffed" with hundreds of transistors and other

1

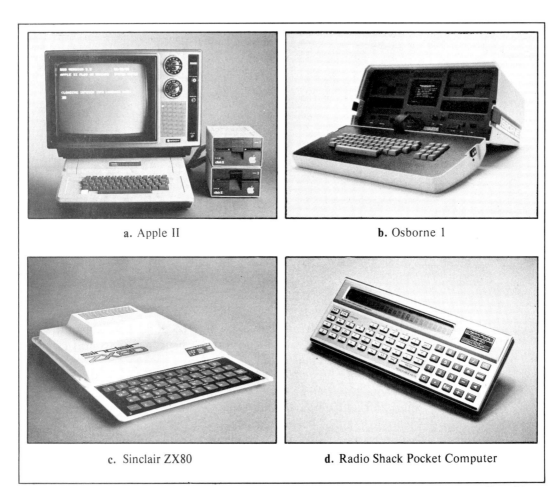

a. Apple II   b. Osborne 1

c. Sinclair ZX80   d. Radio Shack Pocket Computer

Figure 1-1. Microcomputers

Photos by Harvey Schwartz

semiconductor components. Their lower cost made them more afford-
able for universities and businesses. Yet, while this was a tremendous
advance, the age of the consumer computer had to wait for a new technology called *Large Scale Integration* (usually abbreviated LSI). **With
LSI technology, tens of thousands of microscopic electronic circuits
could be crowded into a space an eighth of an inch square.** An LSI
device is pictured in Figure 1-2.

Microprocessor   **The microprocessor is the ultimate LSI component. It contains all
of the circuits needed to create the brain of a simple computer. The
microprocessor is the "computer" within any microcomputer system.**

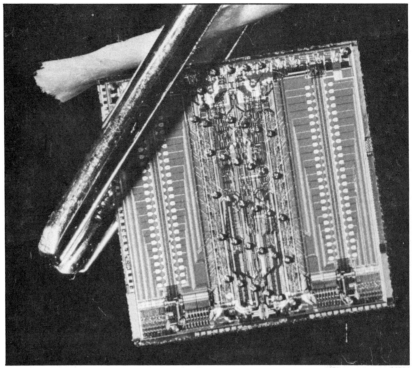

Figure 1-2. LSI device

Photo courtesy of IBM

All of the microcomputers mentioned in this book contain a microprocessor. The microprocessor is put onto a printed circuit card along with other electronic parts that are needed to support the processor, as pictured in Figure 1-3.

The printed circuit card fits inside a container which can be anything from a handheld calculator case (such as the Pocket Computer) to a metal box the size of a footlocker. This container, then, is the "microcomputer."

Interface

Microcomputers can't do much alone. A pocket computer can store basic mathematical formulas like those sometimes used by engineers, and its portability makes it an excellent product to use at construction sites. **But for sophisticated computer applications such as automated**

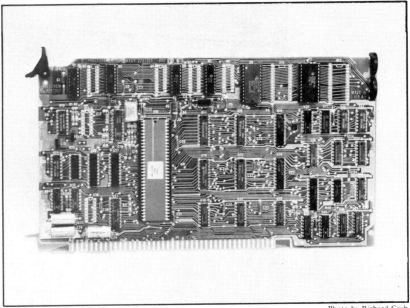

Photo by Richard Cash

Figure 1-3. Printed circuit card

bookkeeping or word processing, the microcomputer must be connected to, or *interfaced** with, other devices.

A microcomputer interfaced to other devices becomes a microcomputer system. This system is really **no different from the idea of a stereo system.** To make a stereo record play you need a turntable, an amplifier, and a set of speakers. **To apply a microcomputer to a specific task, such as word processing, you need a microcomputer, a video display, a printer, and a disk drive, as shown in Figure 1-4.**

---

* One of the difficulties in learning about computers or microcomputers is understanding a certain amount of technical language. While a lot of terminology is pure jargon for its own sake, some terminology is necessary. Remember, English (and for that matter any other language) did not develop in a technological society, and often we are hard pressed to find words or phrases that adequately represent technical concepts. In this book we will introduce you to computer terms, if only to make other computer books understandable.

Photo by Harvey Schwartz

Figure 1-4. A typical microcomputer system with video,
disk drive, and printer

A Microcomputer System

Let us look at the components of the microcomputer system illustrated in Figure 1-4, and see what each component in the system does.

The Microcomputer

System Integration

The computer pictured as part of a typical system is one of the most popular microcomputers. As you can see from the photograph, it has a separate video display and keyboard. **Some microcomputers, such as the Radio Shack TRS-80, have both these components built into the microcomputer package. The trend in microcomputer design seems to be in the direction of *system integration*.** The Osborne 1 computer has two built-in disk drives, in addition to a built-in keyboard and video screen.

One advantage to "going the component route" is that you have a broader choice. The IBM computer can be interfaced to any size or brand of video monitor or television set, black-and-white or color,* while the Radio Shack TRS-80 is fully self-contained.

---

* The distinction between "video monitors" and television sets is explained later in this chapter.

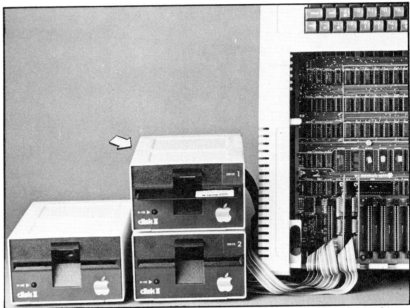

Photo by Harvey Schwartz

Figure 1-5. Floppy disk drive

As with stereos, microcomputer systems with lots of built-in components generally cost less than microcomputer systems with separate components. An Osborne 1, for example, retails for $1795, while an IBM Personal Computer with comparable components may retail for upwards of $4000.

Input and Output
Regardless of whether a microcomputer system is packaged in one box or in a dozen, to understand how the various components interact with each other, you first need to know something about what microcomputers do.

On the most fundamental level, a microcomputer is a machine that receives information (called input), processes it, and then sends it out in a form called output.

Program

Data
There are two kinds of input that a microcomputer, or for that matter any computer, can receive. One kind of input is called a *program* and the other kind is called *data*. A program is simply a list of instructions telling the microcomputer how to act on, or process, the data.

Consider a common program used in many businesses: a "payroll program." This program tells the microcomputer how to calculate pay data and type out paychecks, unaided by human hands.

The data in this case might be employee names or identification numbers and the number of hours they worked during the last pay period. Once it is entered, the microcomputer quickly calculates the amount of pay each employee should receive and prints out the checks. The checks are the *output*.

Every computer program is simply a sequence of numbers. There is nothing special about these numbers, they are just numbers, pure and simple; **a number stored inside a computer may represent a program step, or it may represent data**. It's all a question of interpretation. If the microcomputer fetches a number when it needs a program step, then it simply assumes that the fetched number is a program step. But if the microcomputer expects to receive a number (for example, the number of hours an employee worked), then it assumes that the arriving number is data.

When numbers stored inside the microcomputer are interpreted as numbers or letters of the alphabet — not numbers being interpreted as program steps — they constitute data.

There is nothing unusual about numbers within a microcomputer representing either program steps or data; we all do something similar every day. A number on a piece of paper might be part of a social security number, or it could be a bank check number, the dollar amount of a check, or the dollar amount of a bill. It is only by inspection and interpretation that you can tell what it is. If, while balancing your bank statement, you accidentally read your bank statement number rather than the check amount, you will get a strange and obviously incorrect balance. But there is nothing impossible about making this mistake. Similarly, you will find that there is nothing impossible about a microcomputer reading a data number and interpreting it as a program step, but the results will be very strange.

Numbers represent just a small part of your world. They are the entire world of microcomputers. When you define even a small task for a microcomputer by a program, you will create many hundreds of numbers. By the time you have defined all of the tasks that you want your microcomputer to perform, all these task-defining programs may become many thousands, or even millions, of numbers.

On the surface, at least, this seems to present a problem.

The microcomputer performs any specified task by executing a specific program. The program consists of a sequence of steps, or instructions; each instruction is identified by a unique number.

To get a microcomputer to do even the simplest tasks can take what seems to be an inordinate number of program steps. This is because **a** program not only tells the microcomputer to do the task, but also tells it *how* to do the task as a sequence of program instructions.

To give you an idea of the challenge facing programmers, imagine that you want someone to go to the grocery store. Instead of asking this person to go to the store and giving him or her some money and a grocery list, suppose you had to tell this person how to go to the grocery store in the form of a series of basic human functions, such as:

- Take money and put it in your pocket
- Take grocery list and put it in your pocket
- Put your jacket on
- Go to door
- Open door
- Go to car
- Open car door
- Get into car
- Put key in ignition
- Start car
- Drive out of driveway
- Turn left
- Go three blocks
- Turn right, and so on.

Fortunately, once you've programmed a microcomputer to do something, you can save the program so that the next time you can simply tell it to "go to grocery store" without having to tell it how.

Once a microcomputer has been correctly programmed to do a task, you need never again program it to do that task. Like elephants, microcomputers never forget.

Unlike elephants, however, microcomputers are extremely fast. A microcomputer can go through hundreds or thousands of program steps, or instructions, in less than a second. In fact, microcomputers typically execute single instructions in a time interval ranging from one quarter of one millionth of a second (250 nanoseconds) to 10 millionths of a second (10 microseconds).

Instruction Cycle

Microsecond

Nanosecond

Computer scientists refer to the **amount of time it takes a microcomputer to do a program step** as its *instruction cycle.* The term for a **millionth of a second is a** *microsecond*; a **billionth of a second is a** *nanosecond*. In reading about microcomputers or talking to people about them you will frequently hear the terms instruction cycles, microseconds, and nanoseconds.

Memory

Fast Access Storage

While the microcomputer is incredibly fast, the microprocessor chip inside **a microcomputer only performs one program step at a time. Meanwhile, the other program steps, along with the data, must be stored in internal memory. If the microprocessor is to execute an instruction every few microseconds, then clearly this internal memory must be fast access storage. The microprocessor must be able to fetch the number representing the instruction in even less time than the few microseconds available to execute the entire instruction. Typically, a microprocessor will fetch an instruction number out of** *fast access storage* **in 250 nanoseconds or less.**

Memory Chips

Bytes

A microcomputer's internal memory is stored in integrated circuit chips called *memory chips* **which are similar in appearance to the microprocessor chip.** These chips can either be on the same circuit board as the microprocessor, or they can be on a separate board. Since this type of memory is relatively expensive, **microcomputers usually have the capacity to store from 4096 (called 4K) characters or bytes* of memory to 65,536 (called 64K) characters (1K is equal to 1024).**

The amount of internal memory is an important consideration when selecting a microcomputer. **A machine with less than 16,384 (called 16K) characters or bytes of memory is practically useless because it can only store the smallest programs.**

Because the size of a microcomputer's internal memory is restricted, only program steps and data which the microcomputer is *currently using* can be stored there. **Programs and data which the microcomputer is not currently using are stored externally on some form of cheaper (and slower) bulk storage device.**

Like microcomputers, people have internal and external memory. For example, say you need to make airline reservations. Your mind remembers that this can be done with a phone call, but your mind doesn't remember the airport phone number. The number must be "fetched" from an external storage device, either the telephone book

---

* For reasons which are discussed in great detail in Chapter 4, the program instructions and data that are input and output from a computer are in the form of binary numbers. Binary numbers are numbers that consist of only two digits, a 1 and a 0. These digits are sometimes referred to as *bits*. **In most microcomputers, all the data and program instructions are in the form of 8-digit or 8-bit binary numbers such as 01011001. These 8-bit binary units are called** *bytes.* It is one of those words you'll be seeing a lot of if you continue your interest in microcomputers, partially because it has been popularized as a name for products and publications. The largest circulation microcomputer magazine, for instance, is *BYTE* magazine. There is even a chain of microcomputer retail stores called Byte Shops.

Photo by George Vrana

Figure 1-6. Floppy disk

or directly from the telephone company through an information operator. Then, as you make the reservations, you'll probably write down the flight number and departure and arrival times on a sheet of paper. This sheet of paper then becomes another external storage device.

To carry the analogy a bit further, we could say that the procedure for making an airline reservation, which consists of a number of steps, is actually a program. The airport's telephone number is part of the input data needed to run the program. The flight number and departure and arrival times become output.

Floppy Disk Units

The external bulk storage device pictured in our typical microcomputer system is a *floppy disk* drive.

There are similarities between a floppy disk system and a record player. Both use disks with information recorded on them. Floppy disks are so named because they are soft and bend easily. A floppy disk is shown in Figure 1-6.

Because the disks are floppy, they are housed inside stiff cardboard envelopes to keep them rigid. (See Figure 1-7.)

Photo by Harvey Schwartz

Figure 1-7. Floppy disk envelope

Mini Floppy

There are two sizes of floppy disk: regular ones which are eight inches in diameter, and "mini floppies" which are 5¼ inches in diameter. A smaller, 3-inch diameter floppy disk called a "micro floppy" is just beginning to make its appearance on the market.

While a record has a grooved surface, **the floppy disk has a smooth magnetic surface. On this smooth magnetic surface information is stored as sequences of magnetic pulses.**

Tracks

We will compare data stored on floppy disks with music stored on the surface of a record. The magnetic pulses are recorded along tracks on the surface of the floppy disk. In contrast, music is stored on the surface of a record within a continuous groove. A needle rides the groove in order to position itself, but the floppy disk surface is smooth and has no grooves. The track is an imaginary line along which the magnetic **Read/Write** pulses lie. Information is written onto the track and read off it by a mag-**Head** netic read/write head that is quite similar to the pickup arm of a record player. Of course, the read/write head of the floppy disk unit has no needle since there is no groove to track; instead, it has little metallic pads that can create (write) or sense (read) magnetic pulses on the floppy disk surface.

Until you become a real microcomputer expert, you need not concern yourself with exactly how information is stored on a floppy disk. Most microcomputer users never bother with this information, just as most music lovers never concern themselves with how music is recorded on tape, cassettes, or records. You know that a record, when played, creates music; similarly a floppy disk, when played, creates numbers. You can also write numbers onto a floppy disk, just as you can record music on a magnetic tape or cassette.

For a general understanding of how information is stored on floppy disks, see Appendix A.

Just as you have a record library, you can have a collection of floppy disks. You can buy a prerecorded floppy disk complete with programs, or you can buy blank floppy disks and record your own programs.

Rigid Disk Units

Floppy disks are not the only means of storing programs and data. Big computer systems use large, removable, rigid disks. (See Figure 1-8.)

There is a tremendous variety of removable, rigid disk units on the market. Units are available with every conceivable option, and in a variety of sizes, but they all store information on a much bigger disk that is not a floppy disk. (See Figure 1-9.)

Information is written onto rigid disks, and read off them, via metallic read/write heads similar to those used by floppy disk drives. Both rigid and floppy disk drives place the read and write heads on the end of a moving arm, which is positioned over the track that is to be accessed.

In the case of floppy disk drives, the drive rotates the floppy disk quite slowly, at a rate of one revolution per second, and the **read/write head actually touches the floppy disk surface.** The read/write head cannot touch the surface of a rigid disk since the rigid disk is spun at rates that may exceed 50,000 revolutions per minute. At these high speeds, a read/write head would ruin the disk surface upon touching it, and the disk surface would probably ruin the read/write head. Therefore, **rigid disk drives use a cushion of air to hold the read/write**

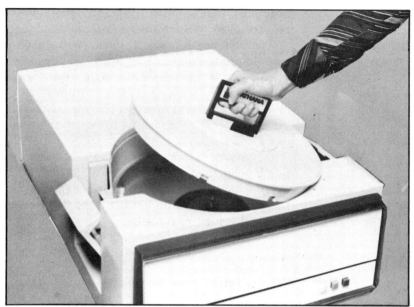

Photo by George Vrana

Figure 1-8. Rigid disk

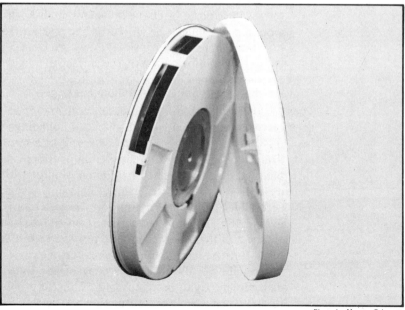

Photo by Harvey Schwartz

Figure 1-9. Stiffness of rigid disk

head only thousandths of an inch above the disk surface. **This is referred to as** *floating* **the heads.**

The distance between the read/write head and the surface of a spinning rigid disk has a lot to do with the amount of data that can be stored on the surface of the rigid disk. As the read/write head is allowed to float closer and closer to the surface of the spinning rigid disk, the magnetized zones representing data on the disk surface can be made smaller. Consequently, more information can be stored on the disk surface.

Unfortunately, when the distance between the read/write head and the spinning rigid disk is very small, dirt in the air becomes a problem. Even particles exhaled by a cigarette smoker are large enough to get between the read/write head and the disk surface, causing data to be read and written incorrectly.

Winchester Disk Drives

In order to solve this problem, another type of disk drive, referred to as **a Winchester disk drive, permanently seals the rigid disk inside a clean, airtight space.** Now the read/write head can be floated just a microscopic distance above the spinning disk surface, and phenomenal amounts of data can be stored on the disk surface.

Winchester disks may store anywhere from 5 million to 100 million characters of information on the surface of a rigid disk no bigger than an eight-inch floppy disk. What is more, the entire unit is relatively inexpensive, costing between $2000 and $6000.

But the large storage capacity and low price of a Winchester disk drive are offset by the disadvantage of not being able to replace the rigid disk as you can with a floppy disk unit or a removable rigid disk unit. Thousands of disks can be loaded into a floppy disk drive or a removable rigid disk drive. The total library of information accessible by these disk drives can be huge, even though only a small part of the library is accessible at any point in time. **In the case of a Winchester disk drive, everything you can ever access is on the disk at one time.**

The fact that disks cannot be removed from Winchester disk drives has a further, less obvious implication.

You should always keep a copy of any information stored on any disk, floppy, rigid, or Winchester. Then, if problems arise, and for any reason you destroy the information on the disk, you still have a back-up copy. You will need some other type of information storage device that you can use to make copies of data stored on the Winchester disk surface. Thus, the Winchester disk drives are less economical than they may appear at first.

Experience has shown that when you weigh the advantages of Winchester disk drives against the disadvantages, the advantages win. Winchester disks have become quite popular in the microcomputer industry among people who find that floppy disks are either too slow or do not store enough information for their needs.

Random Access   **All disk units are referred to as** *random access* **bulk storage devices**. Random access means that you can go directly to any part of the disk in order to read or write information.

Random access is an extremely useful capability in any bulk storage device. The ability to access directly any part of the disk in order to read or write speeds up data access operations.

Logical and   **This is a good point at which to introduce you to a very fundamen-**
Physical   **tal computer concept: the relationship between** *logical* **ideas and**
Records   ***physical* reality.**

Consider one paragraph that is part of a form letter. Let's refer to this paragraph as a *record*.

Physical   On the surface of the floppy disk, this record becomes a *physical*
Record   *record* of five sections of recordings; each section is referred to as a *sector*. Sectors may or may not be contiguous. But why should you worry
Sector   about sectors? Life will become a good deal simpler if you handle information as "paragraphs," or as you might read the information. You
Logical   really want to access information as "logical records," which have
Record   nothing to do with sectors. And that is how a well-designed microcomputer system will let you think. The microcomputer system takes care of finding sectors and linking them together if a record is stored on more than one sector. You do not concern yourself with how many sectors are required by your record, or where the sectors are. You do not even have to know that tracks and sectors exist. **You deal with the "logical idea" of a paragraph and the microcomputer takes care of the "physical reality" of where on the disk this information is physically recorded.**

Thus, when using a well-designed microcomputer system, you can think in terms of logical records, ignoring sectors, tracks, and other such complications. But you should always remember that sectors, tracks, and random access make the floppy disk unit an efficient and fast device to handle bulk information.

The concept of the "logical" versus the "physical" can be extended to cover more than information and records.

Logical units and *physical units* apply in almost every part of any computer system. A logical unit is a piece of information, an idea, or an operation that you will use. A physical unit is the actual physical implementation — the physical reality behind the idea, information, or function.

Records   Suppose you have a number of form letters or a list of names and addresses. Each could be recorded as a logical record on a floppy disk surface. The following shows how the two sets of logical records might be compared:

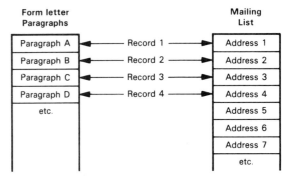

In order to identify a particular piece of information, you must know the logical record number and whether it is one of the form letter logical records or one of the mailing list logical records.

How are you going to identify form letter logical records or mailing list logical records?

Files   Clearly, we do not want to start specifying where on the floppy disk the information is stored; the whole purpose of going to logical records in the first place was to avoid worrying about the floppy disk surface. We therefore combine all of the records into a file. A *file* is simply a collection of one or more records. Once again you deal with logical files and leave the microcomputer the task of determining where the physical file actually exists on the floppy disk surface. Now **you have a "form letter" logical file, where each paragraph is a logical record, and you have a "mailing list" logical file, where each name and address is a logical record.**

Files and records represent the fundamental structure used to store bulk information in all computer systems — from the smallest microcomputer system to the largest mainframe computer system.

This concept of logical files and logical records is not so very different from daily office life. Suppose you need to look at a letter you received from XYZ Corporation. The letter contains price quotes. You could ask a secretary to fetch the 27th letter in the third filing cabinet drawer, but more likely you would ask your secretary to go to the XYZ Corporation file and retrieve the price quotes letter. The XYZ Corporation file is the equivalent of a logical file; each letter in the file is the equivalent of a logical record. Your secretary is the equivalent of the microcomputer intelligence which is capable of accessing a specific item of information given a description of what the information is.

Cassette Storage

If you are a typical microcomputer user, you may feel that you cannot initially afford a floppy disk system. What are the less expensive options? There are cassettes and paper tape.

The cassette units used to store information for microcomputers are exactly the same as the inexpensive cassette players you might buy in any shop. In fact, some microcomputer manufacturers do not include cassette drives in their product line; instead they suggest you use a standard cassette player. Other microcomputer manufacturers do sell their own cassette drives, but these are usually expensive, thinly disguised modifications of popular, inexpensive players.

You must use a high-quality cassette recorder and very high-quality cassette tapes with your microcomputer system, since the microcomputer system is not going to tolerate errors. If you have a glitch in a cassette with music recorded on it, you will have a moment of irritation when you play it back, but that is all. If you have a glitch in a cassette that holds information for your microcomputer, it may render the entire cassette worthless, since the microcomputer will read a block of no numbers or erroneous numbers.

Cassette Interface   **But you cannot simply buy a cassette recorder, set it next to your microcomputer, and expect the two to converse. The actual conversation occurs via appropriate control logic within your microcomputer.**

There are two very different ways in which cassette recorders store information on magnetic tape. The old way was to store information digitally, as a sequence of magnetized dots on the cassette tape surface.

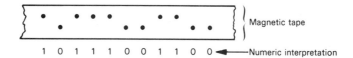

Nearly all industrial cassette recorders store information digitally as illustrated. **Microcomputer cassette recorders** do not record information digitally; rather, they **record information as sounds** — in exactly the same way as they would record voices or any other noise. One particular tone represents a 0 digit while another tone represents a 1 digit.

The principal advantage of using tones to record data is that you can use any cassette recorder as part of your microcomputer system.

Sequential Access

The difference between a cassette unit and a floppy disk unit is that the cassette unit is a sequential (or serial) access device, and the floppy disk unit is a random access device. When we say that a cassette unit is a sequential device, we mean that you cannot jump around on the surface of the cassette the way you can on the surface of a floppy disk. If you wish to access the 25th record on a cassette tape, you must first count your way past the first 24 records. Information stored far into a cassette may take a long time to access — up to 10 or 15 minutes to reach the last record on a cassette.

Cassette Reading and Writing

Because we must sequentially access information on cassettes, it is very difficult to read and write on the same cassette. Suppose, for example, you are storing a list of names and addresses on a cassette tape. This may be illustrated as follows:

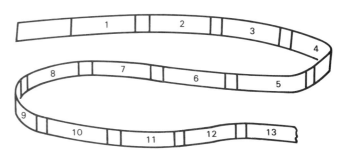

The numbers **13** through **13** represent 13 individual addresses

Now suppose you want to change the third name and address (3). This might seem to be a simple enough job; you simply write the new name and address over the old one.

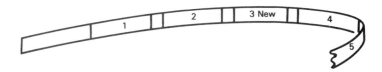

But wait a minute. This could become a very tricky operation. Suppose the new name and address is longer than the old one; you will now erase part of the next name and address.

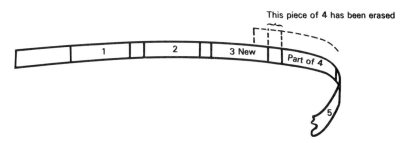

We can get around this problem by reserving the same amount of space for every name and address, irrespective of the number of characters actually in the name and address. Excess characters will be left blank. This may be illustrated as follows:

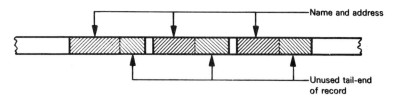

But even this is not an adequate solution, since it demands that your cassette drive mechanism be very precise. Suppose you start rewriting a very small distance too late.

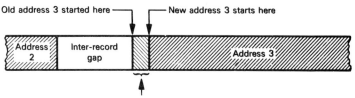

When the microcomputer system reads Address 3 off the cassette, it will pick up the remnant of the old name and address, and you will get a read error. If you start writing too early, you have a glitch at the end of the record, and again you will obtain an error when you read back.

Clearly, writing over previous records is just asking for trouble. Cheap cassette recorders will give you more trouble than expensive cassette recorders because the cheap recorders have imprecise drive mechanisms. But the real problem is that only one error ruins the whole cassette. It does not matter whether this one error occurs frequently or occasionally; in either case it renders the cassette useless.

If you have long records and short records mixed on one cassette, reading and writing on the same cassette become a hopeless task. If each logical record is stored on the cassette tape as a single physical record, you cannot write records of differing lengths into the same space. A longer record will erase part of the next record,

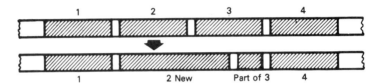

while a shorter record will leave part of the old record, which will be picked up as an error.

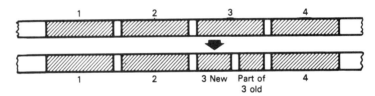

If logical records of various lengths are stored on the cassette tape as a sequence of physical records of equal length, you *could* write and read on the same cassette by breaking up the logical record as we did on the floppy disk. This may be illustrated as follows:

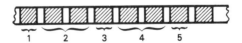

Beginning with this cassette tape, two alternative ways of inserting a new record 3 are

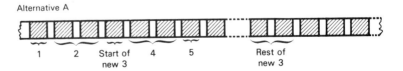

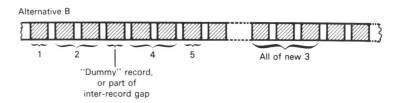

Alternative B

| 1 | 2 | | 4 | 5 | | All of new 3 |

"Dummy" record,
or part of
inter-record gap

The problem with these schemes is that you will grow old watching the cassette wind and rewind. If you have alternative A, the steps that would be needed to read back the record illustrated above are

· Find logical record 2
· Find start of logical record 3
· Wind cassette forward to find the rest of logical record 3
· Rewind to start of logical record 4.

If you use alternative B, you will waste a lot of cassette space. Also, if your records are in order, alphabetically or otherwise, they will soon be in total disorder.

We must conclude that just one cassette unit in your microcomputer system can be very dangerous. You must have at least two cassette units, one to read from and the other to write to.

Paper Tape

There is a bulk storage device that is even more primitive than cassettes: paper tape. At one time paper tape was the only low-cost means of storing computer information, but today cassettes are inexpensive and a good deal faster. There are, nevertheless, many microcomputer systems that use paper tape to store information.

Paper tape, as its name implies, consists of a long, thin strip of paper.

Characters

Information is stored on paper tape by punching holes across the tape.

The principal disadvantage of paper tape is that you will need enormous quantities of it. Although cassette storage densities vary greatly, you would use approximately 2000 feet of paper tape to record the same amount of information as is stored on a single 90-minute cassette, or one side of a single density floppy disk.

Another disadvantage of paper tape is that it takes a long time to record information on paper tape or to read it back. Read and write times will vary between ten and 100 characters per second. While this may seem to be quite fast, cassettes can be written to and read from at between 100 and 1000 characters per second; floppy disk read and write rates range between 1000 and 10,000 characters per second; and with rigid disks, you can read and write at rates in excess of 1 million characters per second.

You must understand the different frames of reference that you will apply to the idea of time once you start working with computers. Why is ten characters per second considered a slow time? Because you will usually read or write hundreds or thousands of characters at a time, and more often than not, you will have nothing to do but watch while the read or write operation occurs.

The Video Display

RF Modulator   In the case of most Apple II and ATARI 400 and 800 microcomputers the video display is a standard television set. The Apple or ATARI computers are connected to it via an *RF modulator* — a matchbox-sized electronic package which is hooked up to the antenna leads of the television. This is the same way that home video games are connected to television sets.

Advantages of using a Video Monitor

Instead of being connected to a television set through the antenna leads, microcomputers can also be directly plugged into a video monitor. There is very little difference in appearance between a video monitor and a television set. The most apparent difference is that the monitor doesn't have a channel selector, **but a video monitor is a great deal better than a television set because it has better resolution**. Smaller characters (letters, numbers, symbols) are easier to read on a video monitor; the lines in computer graphic images will be much sharper. With a television set it is sometimes impossible to distinguish the letter B from the number 8, or the letter M from the letter N. **If you are considering a television screen as your computer display, you should make sure the display is acceptable to you after you have used it for a few days**.

Many microcomputers, including the Osborne 1, the TRS-80, and the Commodore PET, have built-in video monitors.

In addition to resolution, the most important difference between video monitors and television sets is price. If television manufacturers built high-quality television tubes with the resolution demanded by video monitor terminals, your television set could serve as a microcomputer video display with no loss of display quality; but that would mean paying more for the television.

Like television sets, some monitors display only black-and-white images, while others display color. They also come in a variety of sizes, from small four-inch displays to full-size 12-inch displays.

Upper- and Lower-Case Displays

A vital distinction among microcomputers is how they "relate" to their video displays, whether they are monitors or television sets. **Some microcomputers will only display upper-case letters**; others will display both upper and lower case. This plus the number of characters displayed per line (usually 40 to 80) are very important considerations for word processing and other applications where the end result is letters and numbers printed on paper.

Reverse Display

Some displays allow you to reverse the screen so that black characters are displayed on a white background for part or all of the screen. (See Figure 1-10.)

Photo courtesy of Commodore Business Machines, Inc.

Figure 1-10. Reverse video

**Horizontal
Scrolling**   Some displays let you scroll text horizontally or vertically. **Horizontal scrolling lets you look at text lines that are longer than the screen
is wide**. Thus, the screen acts as a window on the line. This may be
illustrated as follows.

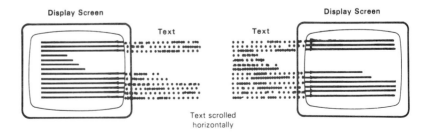

Horizontal scrolling is not a common video display option. Vertical scrolling is much more common. In this case you imagine the text as having more lines than the screen will display; the screen allows you to move the text up and down. This may be illustrated as follows:

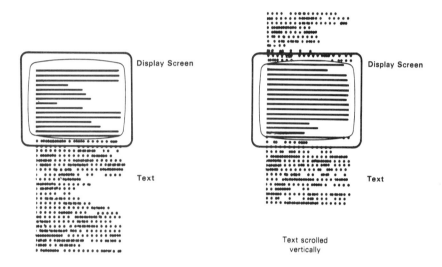

Display Screen

Text

Display Screen

Text

Text scrolled
vertically

There are two ways in which terminals provide vertical scrolling, and one is better than the other. We will describe both.

The less desirable version of vertical scrolling holds all the text which you can display in internal memory. This may be illustrated as follows:

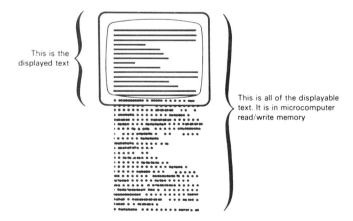

This is the
displayed text

This is all of the displayable
text. It is in microcomputer
read/write memory

If you have this version of scrolling, you cannot scroll above the top or below the bottom of the text currently held in internal memory. If you insert text and overflow the available internal memory, you will simply lose information from the top or bottom of your text.

If your microcomputer has a floppy disk unit, a well-designed scrolling option will connect the floppy disk unit to the internal memory within which displayed text is being stored. Now, if you scroll above or below the text in memory, programs within the microcomputer system will automatically store some of the internal memory text back onto the floppy disk and bring new text from the floppy disk into the microcomputer. To you, text appears to scroll indefinitely. This may be illustrated as follows:

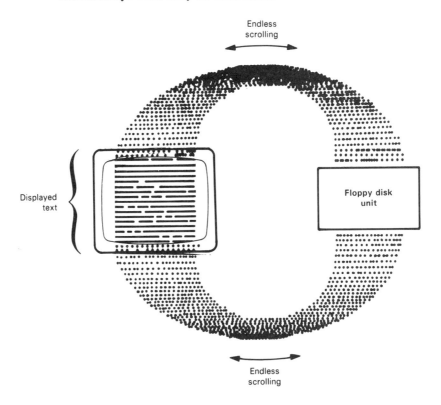

If you insert text when using this more advanced scrolling technique and you overflow the available microcomputer internal memory, the overflowing text will simply get written out to the floppy disk and will not be lost.

Remember that these scrolling options have nothing to do with video display terminal or keyboard; they are options that rely on the entire microcomputer system and the way in which it has been programmed for you.

CRT

VDU

A video display is sometimes referred to as a **Cathode Ray Tube, or** *CRT,* **or a video display unit,** *VDU.* Calling a video display unit a VDU might seem logical enough, but calling it a CRT is meaningless to the average user. CRT refers to the way in which television and video display tubes are built today; cathode rays are used to create displays. In the not too distant future, cathode rays will probably be replaced with cheaper, more efficient technologies; but do not expect terminology to change with technology. Computer scientists will probably refer to video displays as CRTs long after cathode ray video displays have found their final resting place in science museums.

The Keyboard

The video display discussed above is one of the devices microcomputers use to *interface* **with you.** It is through this device that the microcomputer responds, or *talks,* to you. Now we are going to look at **another device, the keyboard, which allows you to enter information, or** *talk* **to the microcomputer.** (In the future a microphone will replace the keyboard on microcomputers, enabling you to literally talk to the machine.)

As with video displays, some microcomputers come with built-in keyboards, while others require separate units. Just about all keyboards have the standard typewriter layout with a few extra keys that are used to control computer operations. For convenience, many keyboards have an additional ten-key numeric pad on the right-hand side. The numeric pad is not important if you are using the microcomputer in some simple operation that does not require a great deal of numeric data entry. In standard data processing applications a great deal of numeric data entry is required, and the numeric pad is a very important feature. A keyboard with a numeric pad is shown in Figure 1-11, and a typewriter-style keyboard is shown in Figure 1-12.

Some keyboards have graphic symbols which can be displayed like any character. You can have a lot of fun using a small microcomputer's graphics capabilities, but graphics are of little value to most data processing applications.

Rollover

For satisfactory use of a microcomputer in most applications, keyboards must have a feature called *rollover.* **If you press a key,**

Photo by Harvey Schwartz

Figure 1-11. Keyboard with numeric pad

Photo by Harvey Schwartz

Figure 1-12. Keyboard without numeric pad

then press a second key before releasing the first key, some keyboards will miss the second key entirely. Keyboards with rollover will not miss the second key. For example, suppose you press the B key, then while the B key is still depressed you press the K key. Now release the B key, followed by the K key. A keyboard with rollover will detect both keys. Fast typists continuously overlap keystrokes and need rollover. They are severely hampered by keyboards without rollover.

Another technique used to make keyboards error proof is to have some storage location within which character codes are stored while

waiting to be transmitted to the microcomputer. This may be illustrated as follows:

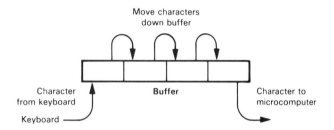

Keyboard Buffer

The storage location illustrated is referred to as a *buffer*. Although the buffer is shown having room to store four characters, a real buffer may have any number of characters ranging from two to eight. A buffer gives the microcomputer more time to handle occasional characters that require long response times.

This raises an obscure aspect of keyboards which we must consider: exactly when is a key going to be detected as depressed? Answering this question is not quite as simple as it sounds. You might assume that pressing a key causes some type of contact to close, at which point the key is considered depressed.

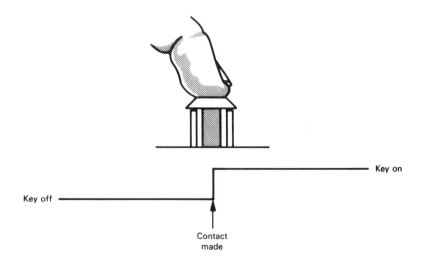

Unfortunately, electrical contacts are not always clean. The simple contact shown above might more accurately occur as follows:

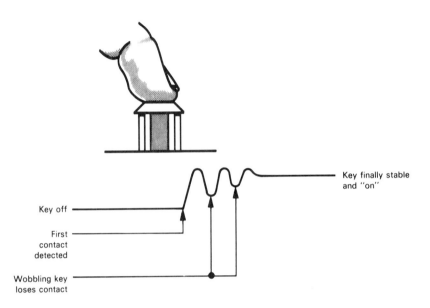

Key finally stable and "on"

Key off

First contact detected

Wobbling key loses contact

Debouncing   The varying pressure of a finger on a key may result in key contact appearing to flicker on and off for some period of time after a key has been depressed. This is referred to as *bouncing*. Any well-built keyboard will contain debouncing electronics. A debounced keyboard will convert a ragged signal to a clean on-to-off signal. This may be illustrated as follows:

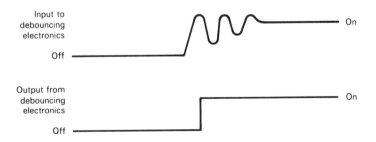

Input to debouncing electronics   On

Off

Output from debouncing electronics   On

Off

Rollover, buffers, and debouncing are electronic options associated with keyboards. It is important that you evaluate mechanical aspects of keyboards.

The normal type of mechanical keyboard has keys which may be conceptualized as follows:

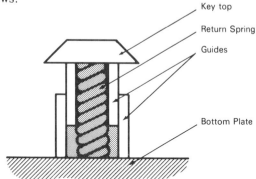

A mechanical switch will have a spring which returns it to the off position. You compress the spring by pushing the switch down. At some point, when you have depressed the switch far enough, an electrical contact is made, at which point the switch is on.

A sturdy mechanical guide must be provided to ensure that when you press a switch it makes a clean descent to the point of electrical contact. A mechanical switch may appear to be very elementary, but it really is not. For example, no one ever presses a switch straight down; invariably, the angle at which your finger touches a switch must be designed with this in mind. Consider also the electrical contact; it might appear that an electrical contact is generated very simply by having metal on the key (or key stem) make contact with metal on the guide (or bottom plate). But this type of dry contact, if not well-designed, will give you nothing but trouble. Even a small amount of corrosion on the metal surfaces is sufficient to render the switch ineffective. Sometimes you can improve inexpensive switches by spraying with a suitable cleaner. But do not do so indiscriminately, since you might find the cleaner attacks the plastic used to construct the switch.

Mechanical keys also have options. The most common option is an audible or tactile click accompanying a key being depressed. The microcomputer does not need a click — the operator does — it is there simply to reassure an operator that the key has indeed been depressed.

A general rule of thumb to follow when buying a microcomputer is to choose a keyboard which has the same size and quality you would expect of a high-quality typewriter. There are less expensive keyboards which might be perfectly adequate if you are not going to spend a lot of time entering information at the keyboard. Such a keyboard is shown in Figure 1-13.

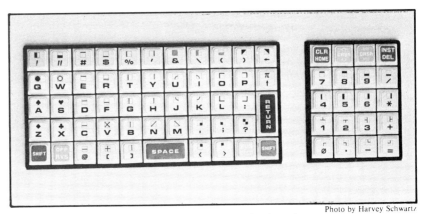

Photo by Harvey Schwartz

Figure 1-13. Compact keyboard

Compact Keyboard

Figure 1-13 shows a very **compact keyboard** that was used on early versions of microcomputers manufactured by Commodore. **These keyboards are adequate for anyone who uses the microcomputer to play games or run small programs that require very little use of the keyboard. However, most people want to make better use of their microcomputers than this.** As a consequence, Commodore no longer manufactures microcomputers with compact keyboards.

Touch Switch Keyboard

Another type of keyboard is called a **touch switch keyboard**. This keyboard appears to have keys printed on the surface of a plastic sheet. When you touch one of these printed keys, the effect is the same as pressing a standard key. **These inexpensive keyboards work on the same principle as the touch switch keys which you may see in elevators**: when you touch the selected floor number the key lights up, but no part of the key moves. **Touch switch keyboards are inadequate in data processing applications since an operator would have to keep his or her fingers hovering over the keyboard.** Fingers can rest on real keys without causing problems, but each time a finger inadvertently touches a touch switch key, it has the same effect as pressing the key.

There are many keyboards on the market, and each has special features or capabilities which you may find relevant or ridiculous. You could replace the keyboard with a typewriter, provided someone builds an appropriate interface for the typewriter.

Interface

And what does an interface consist of?

As with the cassette recorder mentioned previously, if you simply stand your typewriter next to your microcomputer and television set, hitting typewriter keys will have no effect on the television display.

Someone must build the electronics that senses depressed keys and creates appropriate signals, causing the microcomputer and television to know that a key has been depressed.

As you might expect, the keyboard, the floppy disk drive, the video display, in fact, every component of a microcomputer system must have its own electronic interface to the microcomputer.

You can replace a keyboard and video display with a television set and typewriter. (But you would not want to.)

The Printers

The typewriter offers something that a keyboard doesn't: the typewriter prints what you type. In our microcomputer system we show a printer performing this function.

If we substitute a typewriter for the keyboard we can eliminate the printer. So why do people buy printers? One answer is for print speed. Typewriters are clumsy mechanical devices that do not print more than 15 characters per second. The slowest printers are twice that fast, while a fast printer can print 600 lines a minute. A very fast printer will print thousands of lines per minute.

Isn't 15 characters per second fast enough? Clearly, nobody can type that fast. But remember that the printer is not simply going to print what you type. Suppose you are using your microcomputer to compile and print out 200 individualized letters. In this case you would type in the text or body of the letter and the 200 names and addresses. The microcomputer would merge the names and addresses with the text and print out 200 individualized letters (known as computer letters). With no further keyboard input on your part, the microcomputer could also print the names and addresses on the envelopes.

Printing out 200 letters and envelopes at typewriter speed would take several hours during which time your microcomputer could not be used for other tasks.* **By simply substituting a faster printer you can significantly reduce print time and put the microcomputer system to other uses sooner. A printer that prints 150 characters per second — and this is not unreasonable — will print out in six minutes what a typewriter can print out in one hour.**

---

* Some systems have software that allows you to work on one file while printing out another, but this is the exception.

But print speed is not the only reason for separating the printer from the keyboard. When the two are linked, as they are in a typewriter, every time you hit a key you will print a character. Every time the microcomputer prints a character, it will cause a key to be depressed. That means you cannot use the keyboard while you are printing, and conversely, you cannot print while you are using the keyboard.

When the keyboard and printer are mechanically coupled, depressing a key automatically prints a character. However, when the keyboard and printer are disconnected, the microcomputer must be programmed to print back the typed character; otherwise it will not be printed.

Echo   If the microcomputer returns a character to the printer or to the display, it is said to be *echoing* the character.

We have just mentioned an important concept: the independent control of related devices by the microcomputer. The fact that a keyboard and video display unit can be packaged as a single entity does not mean that every time you depress a key an appropriate letter must be displayed. If echo occurs, it is caused by the microcomputer.

In a typewriter the keyboard and the typing element are linked. Every time you press a key the typewriter will print a character, whether you want it to or not. Thus, the microcomputer cannot control echo at a typewriter, and echo is an undesirable characteristic in a microcomputer system.

Types of   While there are simple problems that a microcomputer can solve
Printers   without using a printer — many video games can be played without printers — most serious microcomputer applications require one. Should you decide to buy a microcomputer system, the question isn't whether you should or shouldn't buy a printer, the question is what kind of printer you should buy.

Printers, even more so than microcomputers, come in a bewildering profusion of shapes, types, sizes, and price ranges.

But bear in mind that a printer is a mechanical device. If your microcomputer system breaks down, nine times out of ten the problem will be mechanical, not electronic. Thus, you will want to avoid cheaply constructed printers. You do not need to know anything about microcomputers in order to spot paper guides that are going to break easily, or rollers that do not keep the paper straight. Watch for ribbon advance mechanisms that move the ribbon erratically, and cheap plastic covers that are likely to break.

A printer is one of the most expensive components of any computer system. This has inspired many small companies to manufacture cheap

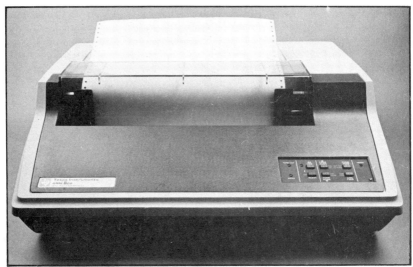

Photo by Harvey Schwartz

Figure 1-14. Matrix line printer

printers that sell for less than $1000. Be careful before you buy one of these printers. You will have to discard most of them within a few months, and then buy the higher quality, more expensive product which you should have chosen in the first place.

There are three varieties of printers. (See Figures 1-14, 1-15, and 1-16.)

· **Matrix printers that generate characters by printing patterns of dots**

· **Printers that work like typewriters and generate typewriter quality printout**

· **Fast line printers that produce solid typewriter-quality characters, but use more expensive print mechanisms to print one whole line at a time.**

Matrix Printers

Most matrix printers generate inelegant characters, but **if you are not concerned with the aesthetics of the characters, matrix printers will give you the best value for your money.** Matrix printers can print special characters or graphic symbols since every character is generated

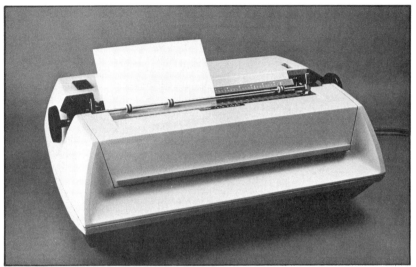

Photo by Harvey Schwartz

Figure 1-15. Letter quality line printer

as a series of dots. Most matrix printers generate characters using a 63-dot rectangle that is seven dots wide and nine dots high. Thus, an upper-case letter A would be printed as follows:

By stretching a single character across many character spaces, a matrix printer can generate large letters suitable for headings and labels.

There are a number of ways in which matrix printers print dots. The simplest way uses tiny hammers triggered by solenoids that strike a ribbon onto paper. Figure 1-17 shows a typical solenoid hammer matrix printing mechanism.

Ink jet printers are printers that shoot tiny drops of ink at the paper. Electrostatic charges deflect the ink drop into the required character dot position. **Ink jet printers are more expensive, but they are very fast. A printer that uses solenoid hammers will not exceed a print rate of 300 lines per minute. Ink jet printers will easily exceed 1200 lines a minute.**

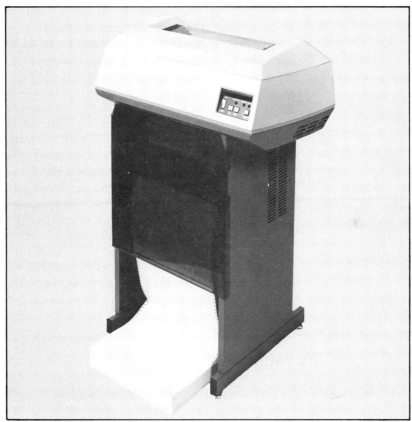

Photo courtesy of Mannesmann Tally

Figure 1-16. Line printer

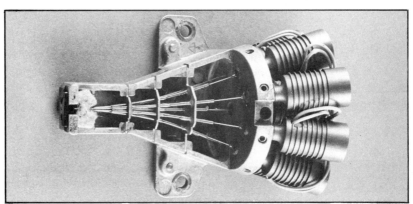

Photo by Harvey Schwartz

Figure 1-17. Solenoid trigger

Solenoid hammer printers and ink jet printers print on ordinary paper. **There are other printers that require special paper; some matrix printers use a special thermal paper which is normally white, but when heated turns blue, black, or some other color.** These printers create dots by pushing a heated point against the paper. Some very inexpensive printers use paper covered with aluminum; they create dots by removing aluminum from the paper surface. These printers create a very strange printout, a metallic-colored paper with black or white dots.

Matrix printers that hit the paper to create dots can be used to create duplicate printouts with carbon paper, just as a typist can type one or more carbon copies of a letter. **Printers that do not strike the paper but use an ink jet or thermal technique print one copy at a time.** You may feel that the ink jet printer's inability to make copies is a disadvantage and that the matrix printer can better supply you with the copies you need. Keep in mind that a matrix printer uses multiple-part paper that is expensive, messy, and troublesome to separate and collate. In addition, the carbon copies are generally of a poor quality. You are better off printing something once, with no carbon copies, and then using a photocopying machine to make copies you need.

Letter Quality Printers

Multi-Pass Printers

A relatively new type of dot matrix printer is the *multi-pass* printer first developed by Sanders Technology Systems, Incorporated. These impact printers, which use the solenoid hammer, **solve the problem of poor quality print by using more than one pass of the printhead per line of type** (the Sanders Media 12/7 printer uses four passes). Prior to each pass, the printhead is moved slightly in a vertical direction so that resulting letters and other characters are filled in. Multi-pass printers give the operator a choice of different type fonts or styles, as well as type sizes. Thus, you can print out a single document with more than one kind of type without stopping the printer to change printheads.

Two of the disadvantages of multi-pass printers are that they are much slower than single-pass printers and that they wear out ribbons faster. These problems are somewhat resolved because these printers give you the option of single-pass printing for documents such as draft copies where print quality is not so important. Another disadvantage (at the time of this writing) is price. Since multi-pass printing is a fairly new technology these machine haven't yet been sold in large enough quantities to bring about significant price reductions.

Daisy
Wheel   **The most common typewriter-quality printers use a *daisy-wheel***
print element. This print element has 96 "petals" on it; each of them
has a character embossed on its tip. The element is rotated until the
required petal is in front of a hammer, which is then fired. In this
fashion, lines are printed one character at a time. Daisy-wheel printers
are reliable, and they generate typewriter-quality printout. But in computer terms they are quite slow, printing between 30 and 45 characters
per second.

High-Speed Line Printers

If you want high quality printout and a lot of it, you will need a line
printer. The least expensive line printers use a steel belt on which all
printable characters are embossed. The belt moves across the paper,
separated from it by a ribbon. Solenoid hammers are fired at the steel
belt when characters are correctly placed, thereby printing characters.

The Teletype Terminal

There is a single physical unit that combines all the additional
capabilities that must be added to a microcomputer in order to have a
microcomputer system; it is the teletype terminal.

The teletype terminal is a very interesting device. It has been around
for more than 20 years and has remained virtually unaltered for this
period. It can withstand the rigors of frequent use better than any other
piece of computer equipment, and there are probably more teletype terminals in use than any other kind of computer terminal. The reason that
teletype terminals are so popular, and so enduring, is that they give you
a little bit of every element you need to support a computer. And they
rarely break down. **Let's take a look at a teletype terminal.**

A teletype terminal, as shown in Figure 1-18, has a keyboard
which you use to enter information into the microcomputer's memory.
It has a printer which can print out information or carry on a dialogue
with another microcomputer. And it has a paper tape reader and punch
which can be used for external storage of programs and data.

Other Components

Just as the most common combination in a stereo system is a turntable,
speakers, and amplifier, **the most common configuration of a**
microcomputer system is a microcomputer with a built-in or separate

Photo by George Vrana

Figure 1-18. Teletype terminal

Photo courtesy of Commodore Business Machines, Inc.

Figure 1-19. Modem

keyboard and screen, a floppy disk drive or cassette, and a printer. However, both of these systems can include a multitude of other components. Two of the more frequent additions to a stereo system are an AM-FM tuner and a tape deck. In this section we will take a brief look at some of the microcomputer components or peripherals which we haven't already covered.

Acoustic Modem

One of the first peripherals you may want to know about is an *acoustic modem.* **This device,** shown in Figure 1-19, **allows you to interface your microcomputer with a telephone.**

An acoustic modem converts the binary signals from your computer into audio frequencies in order to send and receive data.

Why would you want to do this? **With a microcomputer and a modem you can do such things as**

· **Connect to one of the many computer bulletin boards**
· **Join an information utility**
· **Send information directly to another computer.**

Computer Bulletin Board

A computer bulletin board is like an electronic version of the classified section of a newspaper. Anyone with a microcomputer or a simple computer terminal and modem can call into the bulletin board to see what messages are on the board or to leave new messages.

The contents of a bulletin board are determined by the people who use it. For example, the "Family-Forum" bulletin board in Washington, D.C., lists genealogical information and helps people find out more about their families. Another bulletin board, "Kinky Komputer," which originates in San Francisco, is used to make sexual connections.

Information Utilities

An information utility is a larger service and offers many more functions than a bulletin board. While most bulletin boards are free, information utilities require an initiation fee and have fees ranging from $2.50 to as much as $20 per hour.

The two most popular microcomputer information utilities are "The Source," which originates in McLean, Virginia, and "MicroNet," which is in Columbus, Ohio. These utilities offer information and shared software services. Through MicroNet you can read the Associated Press wire and get an electronic version of several newspapers including the *Washington Post* and the *San Francisco Chronicle*. You can play games such as "Adventure," send messages to any of the other MicroNet customers, write programs and save them, get the latest stock information, and many other things.

The third reason for including a modem in your computer system is to send information directly to another computer or terminal. If you are a salesman you may want to be able to send sales reports directly to the home office. Many newspaper reporters already use this technology to log in their stories.

Plotter

A *plotter* **is a special printing device used to output graphs, charts, and pictures.**

Plotters are very expensive and require special software. Unless you have an application that requires this device you will probably not be interested in acquiring it.

Graphics Tablet

With a *graphics tablet* **you can draw pictures on the screen of your computer.** The Apple Graphics Tablet, pictured in Figure 1-20, is used by illustrators to produce record album covers, architectural drawings, and a variety of other graphic designs.

Music Synthesizer

You can program your microcomputer to play music with the addition of a microcomputer music synthesizer, such as the alphaSyntauri shown in Figure 1-21.

Appliance Controller

For about $100, you can buy the BSR System X-10, a device which controls up to 16 wall sockets or light switches in your home from a single location.

Mountain Hardware, an innovative microcomputer firm in Santa Cruz, California, is marketing a plug-in circuit board for the Apple computer which interfaces it to the X-10.

Once interfaced to the X-10, your Apple can be programmed to give you a status report on all the lights, appliances, and locks which are connected to the system. This report can be displayed on the screen as a schematic diagram of the house or it can be a simple listing.

The X-10 utilizes the wiring system of your house. Digital signals are sent from the X-10 to small receiver modules which plug into outlets or replace existing electric switches.

These receiver modules act as intermediary switches between the X-10 and whatever light or appliance you wish to control. In other words, the module plugs into the outlet, and the device or light to be controlled is plugged into the module.

You might use this system to preset the lights and appliances in your house to turn on or off at specified times of the day or week; or you might control the television set in your children's room to regulate the programs they view. Or you could design a security system or a fire alarm.

Speech Synthesizer

Speech synthesizers, such as the Computalker, are still being developed, yet they can say a limited number of words or phrases. They are used mainly for games or educational programs.

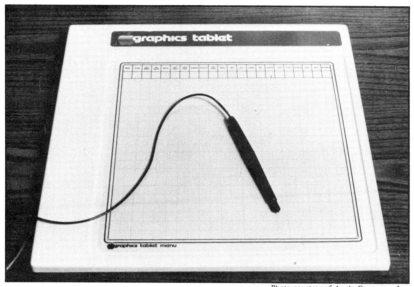

Photo courtesy of Apple Computers Inc.

Figure 1-20. Graphics tablet

Photo courtesy of Syntauri Corporation

Figure 1-21. alphaSyntauri music synthesizer

2
Choosing a Microcomputer

Let's take a look at the many types of microcomputer systems that are available today.

In order to help us in this task, meet Susan Kilobyte, a former computer hobbyist who recently started working as a customer service representative for Ace Products.

Back in 1976, when the microcomputer industry was in its infancy, Susan was one of those fearless few who built her own microcomputer from a kit. Since knowledge is worth money, Susan figured that the time and money she spent building a kit was worthwhile. She ended up with an excellent understanding of microcomputers — and a lot of useless computer hardware collecting dust in her basement.

As a result of various misadventures, Susan Kilobyte no longer had a computer she could call her own. It was music to her ears when she heard Mr. Fogarty, her boss, mumble something about it being time that Ace Products got a computer. Mr. Fogarty owned Ace Products, and whatever Mr. Fogarty said, people at Ace Products did.

"Mr. Fogarty, I know all about microcomputers," Susan said. "In fact, I built my own computer once. I'd love to help you get a computer for Ace Products. These days you can buy some great microcomputer systems for less than $10,000."

But Mr. Fogarty had his own ideas about economical microcomputers. Reaching into his pocket he pulled out a page torn from a magazine.

"I don't know about $10,000 systems," he said. "I'm thinking more about spending a couple of hundred bucks."

In dismay Susan Kilobyte watched Mr. Fogarty lay the magazine page on his desk and smooth out the wrinkles. It advertised **a Sinclair ZX80 personal computer, costing less than $200.**

"Oh, Mr. Fogarty," Susan said. "That's a toy. You can't do a thing with that."

"That's not what the ad says," Mr. Fogarty replied.

"But you need a display. What are you going to use for a display?" Susan asked.

"The ad says I can use a television," Mr. Fogarty replied. "There's that TV set here in my office which I never use. We'll start with it."

"And wherever are you going to store your programs? Or your data?" Susan asked.

"Look, it says right here," Mr. Fogarty stuck his finger into the middle of the ad. "You just use cassette tapes. Get that old tape recorder from the storeroom. Nobody uses it anymore."

"But you'll need a printer. How do you print results?" Susan persisted.

"Printer? Who needs a printer?" Mr. Fogarty asked. "This computer's for Jack. He does all the bookkeeping and all the calculating by hand, and he doesn't get it right every time either. Now the computer can do the calculating, and Jack can write down the results."

"But you don't understand!" Susan Kilobyte wailed. "It doesn't work that way. If you buy a cheap computer, you're just wasting your money."

"Maybe you're right, but if you are, I'm not wasting a whole lot of it," Mr. Fogarty said. "Not like Fred Butler down the road. He bought a computer for more than twenty grand more than a year ago. It still isn't doing anything except taking up space."

UPS delivered Ace Products' microcomputer some weeks later. The ZX80 is the size of a small book. (See Figure 1-1.)

Mr. Fogarty, murmuring approvingly, hovered over Susan Kilobyte, while she unpacked the box, read the accompanying documentation, and then connected the computer to a tape cassette drive and a television set.

Until the computer actually arrived, Jack had looked upon the whole escapade as the type of a folly bosses indulge in when they have nothing better to do. Apart from a comment that "at least Mr. Fogarty was only spending a couple of hundred dollars," Jack had assiduously avoided involving himself in the harebrained scheme. Now that the computer had actually arrived, he continued to keep his distance; but on a couple of occasions, curiosity overwhelmed his suspicions, and he walked in on the computer installation ceremony on a pretext. On the third such visit Mr. Fogarty spoke up.

"Jack," he said, "I think you should stick around. When Susan has taught you how to use this thing, it will be all yours."

"Not that I ever asked for it," Jack replied, but he stayed.

By now Susan had the computer connected to Mr. Fogarty's television set and tape recorder. They were ready to go.

"Where's the computer?" Jack asked.

"Inside here," Susan tapped the box right behind the keyboard.

"That tiny thing? That's a computer?" Jack exclaimed. "I thought computers had switches and lights and things all over them."

"They did," said Susan, "but no more. Actually, a few microcomputers still have front panels with switches and lights," she added, trying to be very precise. "But that stuff is no longer necessary. In fact, it costs more to build a front panel than it costs to build a computer."

"Where's the keyboard?" Jack eyed the ZX80 with deep suspicion.

"Right here. Look." The keyboard appeared to be printed on a piece of thin plastic.

"That's not a keyboard! It doesn't have any keys. It's only a picture of a keyboard," Jack protested.

"It's a keyboard," Susan stated authoritatively. "Some calculators have keyboards like this one. Some elevator switches work like this." Jack was not convinced. "It's cheap," Susan added.

"Yes," Jack said very slowly, agreeing for the first time.

Creating a Program and Making It Work

Fred Fogarty decided that Ace Products' microcomputer should begin earning its keep by helping Jack pay bills. To accomplish this task, Susan wrote a program on a piece of paper, using a programming language. The program had to be very small, because the ZX80 microcomputer does not have much memory in which to store programs.

When Susan had finished writing her program on a piece of paper, she entered it into the ZX80 microcomputer's memory via the keyboard. This is a straightforward process on any modern microcomputer. All Susan had to do was connect power to the ZX80 and start tapping keys. The ZX80 assumes that you are entering a program until you tap appropriate keys telling it that you are doing something else.

Things were not always that simple, and creating a program is a good deal more complex on most large microcomputers. (We will discuss the reasons in later chapters.)

Since Susan's program was short, it did not take her very long to key the whole thing into the ZX80 microcomputer. **When the job was done, Susan touched a control key that said RUN on it. This caused the ZX80 to execute her program.**

Error Message

A message at the bottom of the screen told Susan that there were errors in her program.

Susan first made sure that the program as recorded by the microcomputer was the same as the program she wrote down on a piece of paper. If Susan had pressed the wrong key at some point, the two programs would now differ.

It is easy to look at programs stored in the ZX80, or in any other microcomputer's memory. On the ZX80 keyboard there is a LIST key.

Susan touched this key and there appeared as much of her program as would fit on the television screen.

After carefully examining the program as displayed, **Susan discovered that she had pressed the wrong key in two separate places**. The program as displayed was not the same as the program she wrote.

Susan corrected the program as stored by typing correct words in the place of incorrect ones.

Again, Susan pressed the RUN control key and **again a message on the television screen told Susan that her program had mistakes in it**.

Susan went back to her handwritten program. By now Mr. Fogarty was making Susan nervous, so Susan went back to her office and looked the program over. She promised to call Mr. Fogarty once the program was correct and running.

Debugging

What Susan is doing is referred to as *debugging* a program. Computer programmers refer to errors as bugs; hence the term debugging.

There are many ways in which errors can get into a computer program.

Types of Errors

You might touch the wrong key when entering the program with the keyboard; these errors are the price that Susan and other poor typists pay for their lack of keyboard proficiency.

In addition to keyboard errors, most programs when first written contain simple programming errors, meaning that program statements do not accomplish the task that the programmer intended. This can result fom misunderstanding the programming language, or simply not

keeping track of details. Now the programmer's task is much like a doctor's; given the symptoms the programmer must find the cause. The program must be rewritten to eliminate problems, and corrections must be typed into the computer — making sure that no new keyboard errors are introduced.

Finally, when the program is running and executing correctly, you may well discover that you misunderstood the problem. The program is wrong, not because it contains any program errors, but because you misunderstood the task. And the whole correction cycle begins anew.

Saving a Program   Although Susan's program was short, she did not want to reenter it via the keyboard (and correct keyboard errors) each time the program was to be run. Instead, Susan saved her program on cassette tape. That way she could load it back from cassette tape into the ZX80 memory before running it. In order to save the program on cassette tape, Susan connected the ZX80 microcomputer to the cassette recorder's microphone input, touched the SAVE key and waited.

At a later date she would be able to load her program from cassette tape into memory by connecting the ZX80 to the cassette recorder's earphone outlet and pressing the LOAD key.

As this simple sequence demonstrates, there is really no difference between recording your voice, or a program, on cassette tape. To record your voice, you use a microphone; to record a program, you connect the computer to the tape drive, as you would a microphone.

ROM   Consider for a moment the many tasks which Susan's ZX80 microcomputer performed automatically. All of **the "intelligence"**

that it, or any other microcomputer, displays is derived from programs that someone wrote and built into the microcomputer as a permanent part of the machine**. These programs are stored in Read-Only
Memory (usually referred to as ROM). A read-only memory, as its
name implies, can have its contents read, but can never be written into.
The contents of a read-only memory are defined when the device is
manufactured.

System Software

**Applications
Software**

**Every microcomputer has built-in programs that give the
microcomputer its intelligence. In small microcomputers like the
ZX80, all of these built-in programs are provided in ROM. Larger
microcomputers have additional programs on floppy disk or cassette
that are automatically read into the microcomputer's read-write
memory and executed as needed. These programs are collectively
referred to as the microcomputer's *system software*. In contrast, the
term *applications software* is used to describe programs you write (or
someone writes for you) to make the microcomputer perform your
tasks.**

At this point there is nothing more you need to know about a
microcomputer's system software other than the fact that such programs exist. Later, we will describe in more detail the functions performed and the qualities you should seek in system software.

Running a Program

By the time Susan got her program working properly, the microcomputer had ceased to be a novelty, and Mr. Fogarty was no longer
demanding that he be present when anything happened — a development which, as far as Susan was concerned, had not come a day too
soon.

Jack's suspicions of the microcomputer were as strong as ever, but he decided that he had better cooperate. So he sat down with Susan, resigned to doing his best.

Susan's program created a list of account information for everyone who routinely sold goods or services to Ace Products. The list was stored on cassette tape. Susan used two cassette tapes, one to hold her program, the other to store account information.

Jack brought a stack of bills and deposited them next to the microcomputer. Here's what Susan had to do. First she loaded her program cassette into the cassette drive. She then connected the cassette drive monitor outlet to the ZX80 micocomputer's earphone input, pressed the ZX80 LOAD key, and loaded her program from the cassette into the ZX80 memory.

Once she loaded her program into memory, Susan had to rewind and remove the program cassette. Then she had to place her account information cassette in the cassette drive.

Susan's program was then ready to run. Her program read account information off the cassette for the first account and displayed it on the television set. Susan updated information for this account showing new bills received and checks paid. Susan was now ready to write the updated account information back to a cassette; this she could do in one of two ways: she could have one cassette per account, or she could keep information for all accounts on a single cassette.

Let's look at the trade-offs facing Susan, depending on which strategy she selects.

Back-up Data   If Susan decides to have one cassette tape per account, then she can, if she wishes, rewrite the updated account information back to the same cassette from which she has initially read the account information. Why? Because rewriting the information back to the same cassette would be equivalent to erasing everything that was on the cassette and putting all new information onto it. Therefore, no misalignment would be likely to occur. But Susan would not be likely to rewrite new information on the old cassette for a totally different reason: she needs a back-up cassette. What if a cassette is damaged? Or what if she puts the wrong cassette into the drive at some point? **In all data processing applications it is imperative that you keep copies of all data to guard against such disasters**. Instead of writing updated account information back over the old account cassette, Susan must write the new information to a new cassette.

The problem with having a separate cassette for each account is that Susan would soon have a closet full of cassette tapes. For example, if Ace Products had 200 active vendors, Susan would need 400 tape cassettes. The cost of the cassettes would exceed the cost of the microcomputer. But far worse, Susan would be faced with problems making sure that she properly labeled all her cassettes. Moreover, she would be presented with an unreasonable number of opportunities to place the wrong cassette in a cassette drive and throw the entire payables operation into disorder.

Susan's alternative solution is to store information for a large number of accounts on a single cassette. Suppose, for example, Susan could store information for 50 accounts on a single 90-minute cassette tape. Information for 200 vendors could then be stored on four cassette tapes, in which case eight cassettes would suffice if Susan maintained back-ups.

Susan chooses to store information for 50 accounts on a single cassette tape. This decision is not based on her knowledge of computer operations; rather, Susan is frightened of what Mr. Fogarty will say when presented with a $1200 bill for 600 cassette tapes.

But after Susan put information for 50 accounts on a single cassette tape, she experienced a nightmare when she ran the program.

Handling the first account was easy; Susan placed the ''New Data'' cassette in the tape drive, read the first account information off the tape, and removed it. Susan then placed a blank cassette in the tape drive and wrote updated information for the first account at the beginning of this blank cassette tape. This became the new ''New Data'' cassette. The old ''New Data'' tape became the ''Old Data'' tape.

Susan carefully took out the new New Data tape without rewinding it. She wanted to put it back in the drive and write the second account's new information immediately after the first account. Susan tried removing the Old Data cassette without rewinding it, so she could immediately read information for the next account. This method worked most of the time, but sometimes she did not stop the tape quickly enough after reading one record. To reposition the tape Susan had to rewind it and read each record up to the one she now needed.

By the time Susan and Jack had looked at five accounts, Jack was convinced that his suspicions of the microcomputer were well-founded. Waiting for the cassette drive was getting downright tedious.

''I don't like this microcomputer thing,'' Jack grumbled. ''I could do the job faster by hand.'' And for the balance of accounts, he proved his point by doing things the old way while the microcomputer did them the new way. With each new account Jack got further and further ahead of the microcomputer.

At this unfortunate moment Mr. Fogarty walked in to see how things were going.

"Just fine," Jack said, beaming from ear to ear. "I am doing it by hand faster than the microcomputer." Mr. Fogarty laughed nervously, unsure whether Jack was joking or serious. His laugh turned to a sour grin when he realized that Jack was serious.

Susan explained the problem. With one cassette drive they had to wait forever while she swapped cassettes. "This," Susan explained, "was because the microcomputer had to read an account's data, update it, then write the data out."

"We need two cassette drives," Susan said, "and the ZX80 doesn't allow two cassette drives. With two cassette drives I could read old records from a cassette in one drive, and write new records to a cassette in the other. Then I could at least keep up with Jack, even if I didn't get ahead of him."

Mr. Fogarty decided to think about this problem. And during the next few weeks Jack presented Mr. Fogarty with an additional problem.

Jack hated the ZX80 keyboard.

Touch Switch Keyboard
Susan explained that it was a *touch switch keyboard*. Touch a key and the microcomputer senses the touch. Jack knew how to type, and typists rest their fingertips on the typewriter keys. When using a typewriter, this causes no problems, but Jack could not rest his fingertips on touch switch keys, because every touch became a keystroke.

Touch switch keyboards are fine for typists who only use one finger, like Susan, but as far as Jack was concerned, the ZX80 had to go.

And there was the problem of a printer. Reading information off the television screen in order to write checks was very tedious. If the microcomputer was going to keep records, why couldn't it type checks? Furthermore, there was no way Jack could keep all of his accounts payable records on cassette tapes, with no printed copy. What if a cassette tape was damaged? What if the computer stopped working? He insisted on having ledgers that he could read. And he knew that the auditors would insist on such printed records. Thus, Jack had the choice of taking all the information stored on cassette tape and writing it out by hand — which defeated the purpose of having a microcomputer — or convincing Mr. Fogarty to buy a printer for the microcomputer.

It was becoming clear to Mr. Fogarty that you could not buy a microcomputer for less than $200 and do data processing with it.

Jack felt that the sensible thing to do would be to take the dumb little computer and throw it out. He commended Mr. Fogarty for only wasting a couple of hundred dollars on his computer foolishness.

But Mr. Fogarty was not convinced.

True, Susan Kilobyte had not succeeded in creating a successful payables system, but computers, like any other product, must offer better models for more money, and Ace Products had certainly started at the bottom end of the economic spectrum. Moreover, Susan had warned Mr. Fogarty that the ZX80 was great for learning about microcomputers, but it was incapable of handling real data processing.

So Mr. Fogarty took the little ZX80 microcomputer home and spent a few evenings playing with it. That was sufficient to teach him what Susan had been saying about computers and programming. He was now ready to explore the market — with Susan Kilobyte's help.

All Those Microcomputers

Anyone buying a microcomputer for the first time will probably be overwhelmed by the variations and options he or she sees in every storefront or magazine advertisement.

Mr. Fogarty bought a microcomputer for $200; Susan Kilobyte told him there were some relatively inexpensive systems available for $10,000.

How do you even begin to make sense out of this chaos? Must you spend a year getting educated, or simply take your chances?

Fortunately, microcomputers can be separated into categories, and that simplifies the selection process. Unfortunately, you can start with almost any category of microcomputer, then buy *options,* virtually without limit, until you have priced yourself into a more expensive category.

Microcomputer Categories

Microcomputer systems can be categorized by price and design.

The type of microcomputer you get will depend on what you are willing to pay; but **do not assume that any simple relationship exists between price and system capabilities**. Five thousand dollars will not necessarily buy twice the microcomputing capability that $2500 will buy. The $2500 microcomputer may, in fact, give you more computing power than a system costing twice as much. On the other hand, you can rest assured that all microcomputer systems that cost more than $10,000 offer greater capabilities than any microcomputer system costing less than $1000.

There are a number of reasons why you cannot always measure a microcomputer system's performance by its price. Some reasons are very legitimate, others are not.

The illegitimate reasons first. Occasionally companies charge a lot of money for their product simply to see what the market will bear; but in the microcomputer industry, these people are rare. The problem exists more frequently at the inexpensive end of the spectrum. Inexperienced people, who do not understand the cost of doing business, offer products for ridiculously low prices, until they declare bankruptcy. It is easy enough to avoid buying an overpriced product, but be wary of products that look incredibly cheap. Research the company. They may be offering an excellent value (as is the case with the new integrated computers), but on the other hand, they may be neophytes who do not know what they are doing. Inform yourself of the company's financial organization. What about the people in the company? Are they reputable? Do they have a good record?

It is extremely dangerous to buy products at bargain prices from new companies run by people with no funds or experience in operating successful businesses.

There are, however, legitimate reasons why equivalent products may have very different retail prices.

Companies with superb reputations for quality, service, and support usually charge more for their product. Hewlett-Packard and Apple Computer are two obvious examples. Many people are willing to pay more for a product manufactured by one of these two companies, simply for the security of dealing with a manufacturer that looks after its customers.

Flexibility of design is another factor that has a big impact on price.

A small microcomputer system that has been designed to be expanded to a big microcomputer system is going to cost more than an equivalent small microcomputer system without the expansion capabilities. The expandable system has been designed with features that cost money but are of no use until you expand the system.

If you know that you are going to buy a small system now, but expand it in the future, then buying a less expensive system that is hard to expand makes no sense.

On the other hand, if the system you buy now will likely serve your needs for the next few years, there is no point in paying more for expansion capabilities that you will never use.

Many of the more expensive microcomputer systems have special capabilities; these include high-resolution color graphics, the ability to communicate with a wide variety of mainframe computer systems, high-speed arithmetic processing, or the ability to handle analog signals. Clearly, you do not want to pay for these options unless you are going to use them; but you must pay for these options if you need them.

Decide what you want a microcomputer to do for you, then buy a product that has been designed to meet your needs. Microcomputers are now so inexpensive that it no longer makes sense to buy the wrong system, in anticipation of it becoming the right system some time in the future.

Let's see how Susan Kilobyte resolved her problems.

"Okay," Mr. Fogarty said to Susan, "So I didn't know what I was doing when I got this little thing." He stuck his finger in the middle of the ZX80 keyboard. "Tell me what other equipment is available."

"Don't be so hasty," Susan replied. "Buying that little ZX80 was $200 well spent. Now you know what microcomputers are all about. I would classify this as an introductory microcomputer," she continued, "it's great for teaching you what microcomputers are all about, but don't count on it for anything more."

"Is this as small as they come?" Mr. Fogarty asked.

Handheld
Microcomputers

"No," Susan replied. **"There are** also **handheld microcomputers** that fit in your pocket and look like programmable calculators."

"What *is* the difference between a handheld microcomputer and a programmable calculator?" Mr. Fogarty asked.

"The way you program it; nothing else," Susan replied. "Programmable calculators use strange key sequences, while handheld microcomputers are programmed using BASIC, the same language used to program most larger microcomputers."

"Then what's the difference between an introductory microcomputer, such as this thing, and a handheld microcomputer?" Mr. Fogarty continued.

"You can't put a television set into your pocket," Susan answered. "Pocket microcomputers contain little displays that show you one line of a program or data. It's really all a question of packaging. Pocket microcomputers are great for engineers, scientists, and people who have complicated problems that need to be solved. When we go look at one, you'll see why they are not good for anything else."

"What other kinds of microcomputers are there?" Mr. Fogarty asked.

"There are general purpose microcomputers, and there are microcomputers that have been designed for some specific application."

Specific Applications

"Like a payroll microcomputer?" Mr. Fogarty continued.

"No," said Susan. "There are microcomputers for games and home entertainment. There are microcomputers for industrial control applications. That is what I mean by *specific applications*. If you want to play video games and a simple television set attachment is not good enough, then get yourself a home entertainment microcomputer. But, if you want a microcomputer to control machines on a shop floor, then buy something that has been designed specifically for that task. But for general computing, with a few games on the side perhaps, you should buy yourself a general purpose microcomputer."

Mr. Fogarty had been reading about different systems in magazines, but he was not yet satisfied. "It sounds to me like most microcomputers fall in the general purpose category," he continued.

General Purpose Microcomputers

"Yes," Susan replied, "but **you can divide general purpose microcomputers into three groups — high-end, low-end, and integrated products.**"

"High-end microcomputers are what you buy if you know right from the start that you are going to need a big computer, right?"

"Yes," Susan replied, "and you are better off buying a low-end product if you know that you will never need the big system."

"What about integrated microcomputers," Mr. Fogarty continued, "where do they fit in?"

"They are really low-end microcomputers that are packaged into small portable units with limited expansion capability. Integrated microcomputers also cost less."

"You know," Mr. Fogarty said, "these microcomputers don't look so new to me. They look just like things people used to sell years ago as computer terminals. What's the difference?"

"Computer terminals have been designed to communicate with big computers. It's like taking the television set and keyboard from your ZX80 and making that one unit, while the computer becomes a separate unit. Actually," Susan continued, "there no longer is much difference between a terminal and microcomputer. The terminal has extra communications capabilities which you should pay for if you need them, but not otherwise."

"Well, let's go shopping," Mr. Fogarty said.

And off they went.

Handheld Microcomputers

**Radio Shack
Handheld
Microcomputer**

Susan took Mr. Fogarty to a Radio Shack store and showed him **the Radio Shack handheld microcomputer**. Actually it **is a Sharp handheld microcomputer built in Japan but sold by Radio Shack in the United States. (See Figure 1-1.)**

"It sure looks like a programmable calculator," Mr. Fogarty said.

"Yes, but you program it in BASIC. And see, here is a display." Susan pointed to the glass strip at the top of the microcomputer.

"This little display shows you one line of a program, one line of data input, or a single line of results. That's why it's great for engineers, but not so good for general computing. Usually you will need to see more than one line of a program. And when you run the program, it's easier to have a full screen for entering information and getting the results back."

"But it sure is a handy little thing," Mr. Fogarty mused as he paid the price of the microcomputer and slipped it into his pocket.

"You do a lot of technical work. I bet it will be a real good investment," Susan said.

There are still very few handheld microcomputers on the market, but many can be expected in the future. In addition to Radio Shack, QUASAR and Panasonic produce a handheld microcomputer.

Introductory Microcomputers

"Does my little ZX80 have competition?" Mr. Fogarty asked.

"Well, yes and no," Susan replied. "Micro Ace makes exactly the same product as Sinclair, and there are many borderline microcomputers that cost a little bit more. It really is quite hard to tell where introductory microcomputers end and small general purpose microcomputers and video game microcomputers begin."

"Well, we're not going to buy a microcomputer to play games, but let's take a look anyway," Mr. Fogarty said.

Video Game Microcomputers

**Radio Shack
Color Computer**

"There is a video game microcomputer right here in the Radio Shack store." Susan pointed to a Radio Shack color computer. (See Figure 2-1.)

"Why is this a video game microcomputer?" Mr. Fogarty asked. "For that matter, what separates any video game microcomputer from

Photo by Harvey Schwartz

Figure 2-1. Radio Shack Color Computer

general purpose microcomputers?"

"Not a lot, really." Susan replied. "Video game microcomputers give you color television displays, game handles, and program cartridges; these all cost money and don't help you handle accounts payable."

Susan went on to explain that **using a color television for a display makes no sense unless you plan to play games.** Televisions create poor displays; they are hard to read. A color television gives you a poor display in color. **For a business application you are better off spending the extra money on a black-and-white monitor,** not on a color television set.

Game handles, also called "joy sticks," allow you to control the display. Game handles move a paddle when you are playing "Pong™," or a laser gun when you are playing "Space Invaders™." But game handles serve no useful purpose in business applications, and they cost money.

Game programs frequently are sold in small plastic cartridges that plug into the microcomputer. Game programs could just as easily be sold on cassette tape, but you cannot copy a cartridge (at least not unless you really know what you are doing), while any novice can copy a cassette tape. Also, game cartridges are better than tape cassettes at taking the type of abuse children can subject them to.

Products that incorporate color television displays, game handles, and programs in plastic cartridges should be treated as video game microcomputers. The designers clearly had home entertainment in mind when they designed the microcomputer.

"You mean business applications don't need color?" Mr. Fogarty asked suspiciously.

"Business applications can make good use of color displays," Susan replied, "but if you have the choice of good resolution on a black-and-white monitor, or bad resolution on a color television set, you should choose good resolution on the monitor every time. If you want color, buy a color monitor for a business application; do not buy a color television set."

"That makes sense." Mr. Fogarty said thoughtfully.

"What other video game microcomputers are there?" Mr. Fogarty asked.

Commodore VIC Computer

"**Commodore makes the VIC,**" Susan replied, "and the ATARI microcomputers were all designed for games. **The ATARI 400 and the ATARI 800 computers** are among the best video game microcomputers around." (See Figures 2-2 and 2-3.)

ATARI Microcomputers

Video game microcomputers have not sold well because there is no big market for them. People won't pay $1000 or more for a microcomputer when they can get an attachment for their television sets for less than $200. All of the video game microcomputer manufacturers are

Figure 2-2. Commodore VIC

Photo by Richard Cash

Figure 2-3. ATARI 800 Home Computer

now trying to market their products for business applications, or for the education market; but they are having little success. General purpose microcomputers do a better job in business applications, and people make better teachers.

General Purpose Microcomputers

There are innumerable general purpose microcomputers on the market. We will not attempt to describe them all, brand by brand. To do so would require a book larger than this one. Instead, we will look briefly at some of the most popular models, pointing out a few significant features associated with each.

If you are seriously considering buying a general purpose microcomputer, then consult the *Business System Buyer's Guide* by Adam Osborne, Osborne/McGraw-Hill, 1981. This book summarizes a variety of products and gives a sensible assessment of the purchase of a microcomputer system.

Low-End General Purpose Microcomputers

Apple II Microcomputer Susan spent most of her time showing Mr. Fogarty **low-end general purpose microcomputers**. These **are by far the most popular** microcomputers, and Susan was sure that Mr. Fogarty would end up buying one of them.

TRS-80 Microcomputers Susan showed Mr. Fogarty **the Apple II (see Figure 1-1), the old TRS-80, and the newer replacement from Radio Shack, the TRS-80 Model III. (See Figures 2-4 and 2-5.)**

Photo by Harvey Schwartz

Figure 2-4. Radio Shack TRS-80

Photo by Harvey Schwartz

Figure 2-5. Radio Shack TRS-80 III

Commodore PET and CBM 2001 Microcomputer

Susan also showed Mr. Fogarty an old Commodore PET, plus the newer replacements, the PET 2001 and the CBM 2001 microcomputers. (See Figure 2-6.)

Apple, Radio Shack, and Commodore control most of the microcomputer market. They do not necessarily have the best products, but because they were the only companies who marketed aggressively and operated in a businesslike fashion when many microcomputer manufacturers were fly-by-night, or could not afford to promote their products properly, these three became very successful.

"Should I buy one of the big three?" Mr. Fogarty asked.

"Not necessarily," Susan replied. "Your decision will depend, in the end, on which computer comes with the program you like best."

"If I do buy one of the big three," Mr. Fogarty said, "which is the best?"

"There is no 'best'," Susan replied.

Susan explained to Mr. Fogarty that when a microcomputer is adequate for your needs, it makes no sense to compare capabilities which you will never need.

Many people point out that the early Radio Shack TRS-80 was a very delicate computer, while the early Commodore PET was extremely difficult to program or to use. Apple would have everyone forget that they once made the Apple I microcomputer.

Photo courtesy of Commodore Business Machines

Figure 2-6. Commodore CBM and PET

The microcomputer industry is moving very rapidly. Radio Shack, Commodore, and Apple have all kept pace with industry movement. Radio Shack no longer sells the original TRS-80 because it would be inadequate in today's market. Similarly, Commodore no longer sells the original PET, nor does Apple sell the Apple I. The Apple II will likely be looked upon with scorn in the not too distant future.

An interesting sidelight about Apple, Radio Shack, and Commodore microcomputers is that originally they were products outside the mainstream of microcomputer systems.

S-100 Bus **Early microcomputers were all general purpose products. Most of them were close approximations of each other, sharing the same microprocessor (called the 8080A) and interchangeable electronics. The interchangeable electronics depended on something called the S-100 bus.**

A microcomputer *bus* is an electronic highway which individual modules of a microcomputer use to transmit information back and forth between each other. In theory, all microcomputers that use the S-100 bus have interchangeable electronics; you could take a module (or a single printed circuit card) from one microcomputer and use it in another. Unfortunately, this does not always work.

Some microcomputer manufacturers started to use the Z80 microprocessor, which is, in fact, an 8080A with additional capabilities. Of the three most popular microcomputers, only **Radio Shack uses the Z80 (but not in its color computer), while both Apple and Commodore use the 6502 microprocessor. Neither Apple, Commodore, nor Radio Shack uses the S-100 bus.**

Insofar as programming is concerned, an operating system program called **CP/M (which we will describe later) became a standard for all microcomputers that had 8080A or Z80 microprocessors in them.** CP/M became very popular because programs were written to run using CP/M, rather than to run on a particular microcomputer. Differences between the microcomputers were resolved by making CP/M run on each model.

But **none of the three major manufacturers, Apple, Radio Shack, or Commodore, offered CP/M with their microcomputers.** Other people have now made it possible to run CP/M on Radio Shack and Apple computers, but not on Commodore computers.

A number of small microcomputer manufacturers continue to flourish because they build products that use the S-100 bus and CP/M. Most of the microcomputers manufactured by these smaller companies would now be classified as high-end, general purpose microcomputers.

High-End General Purpose Microcomputers

**Radio Shack
TRS-80 Model II
Microcomputer**

**Commodore
CBM 8000
Microcomputer**

Apple, Commodore, and Radio Shack also have products which could be classified as high-end, general purpose microcomputers. Radio Shack has been in this market the longest of the big three, with its TRS-80 Model II.

Commodore entered the high-end, general purpose market more recently with the CBM 8000 series of microcomputers. These are very capable machines with wide screens and plenty of power. (See Figure 2-7 below.)

Apple was the last of the big three to enter the high-end, general purpose market; they did so with the Apple III, which still has gone largely untested. (See Figure 2-8.)

None of the high-end, general purpose microcomputers offered by the big three uses the S-100 bus or the CP/M operating system. There

Photo courtesy of Commodore Business Machines

Figure 2-7. CBM 8000 series computer

Photo courtesy of Apple Computer, Inc.

Figure 2-8. Apple III

are, however, a large number of smaller microcomputer manufacturers whose high-end, general purpose products use CP/M and S-
100 bus.

S-100, CP/M Compatible
General Purpose Microcomputers

Cromemco

Cromemco sells relatively expensive, really high-end microcomputers;
they use a slightly modified variation of the S-100 bus. CP/M is not a
standard Cromemco product, but their microcomputers will run the
CP/M operating system.

Vector
Graphic

Vector Graphic is another company with an S-100 bus product; all of
their microcomputers are sold with CP/M.

Digital
Microsystems

Digital Microsystems is a small company with a large reputation,
particularly for the quality of their hardware. They build a microcomputer with a pair of floppy disk drives enclosed in a single box. The
product uses a single board computer and runs CP/M. A variety of pe-

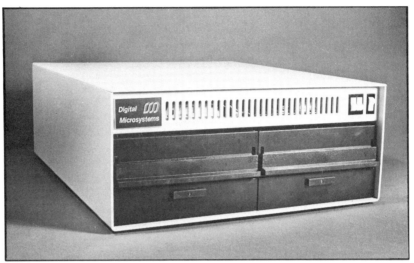

Photo by Harvey Schwartz

Figure 2-9. Digital Microsystems microcomputer

ripheral units manufactured by other companies can be used with the Digital Microsystems microcomputer. (See Figure 2-9.)

Altos   **The Altos Microcomputer** is very similar to the Digital Microsystems product. So is the Altos reputation. However, Altos is a larger company with a broader product line. Recently, Altos announced some low-end, general purpose microcomputers. (See Figure 2-10.)

Morrow Designs Thinker Toys   **Morrow Designs builds a variety of peripheral units that can be used with other S-100 bus compatible microcomputers**. But as of 1980, Morrow Designs did not build the microcomputer themselves. Morrow Designs has a particularly good reputation for the quality of their hardware; their products are frequently sold under the name "Thinker Toys."

North Star   Of the first crop of microcomputer manufacturers, North Star is one of the few survivors. From a humble beginning in a Berkeley storefront (and with the unlikely name of Kentucky Fried Computers), North Star has become one of the largest manufacturers of high-end S-100 bus compatible microcomputers. North Star has its own operating system, but their microcomputers will also run CP/M.

There are probably hundreds of small companies that manufacture S-100 compatible microcomputers operating under CP/M. We could not possibly list all of them. The companies mentioned are just some of the well-known names.

Photo courtesy of Altos Computers Corp.

Figure 2-10. Altos microcomputer

Other High-End, General Purpose Microcomputer Systems

There are two high-end, general purpose microcomputer systems which need to be given special mention.

Texas Instruments DS/1 Microcomputer

Texas Instruments builds the DS/1, which is an upgrade of their old 771 terminal. The DS/1 microcomputer is a very fine product with the advantage of being supported by the Texas Instruments service organization. (See Figure 2-11).

Alpha Micro Systems Microcomputer

Alpha Micro Systems builds the "Cadillac" of high-end, general purpose microcomputers. Their product is so high-end that it belongs in the ranks of minicomputers; nevertheless, it has been sold mostly within the microcomputer market. Most Alpha Micro Systems microcomputers are sold with rigid disks because the computer is considered too powerful to waste on floppy disk drives. The computer does use the S-100 bus, but its central processing unit is almost identical to

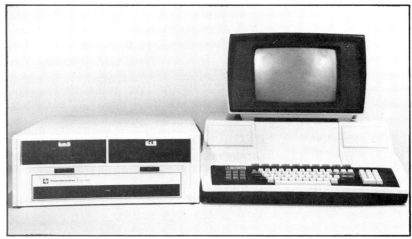

Figure 2-11. Texas Instruments DS/1

the PDP 11, the most widely used minicomputer in the world, manufactured by Digital Equipment Corporation.

Integrated Microcomputer Systems

Osborne 1
Microcomputer

Susan took Mr. Fogarty to a computer store to look at an Osborne 1 microcomputer. They saw that it was a unit roughly the size of a briefcase which contains a small screen and a pair of floppy disk drives. A cover over the screen and the disk drives opened to reveal a full keyboard on the inside. The unit costs half of what an equivalent low-end, general purpose microcomputer costs, and the Osborne 1 computer is sold with a large number of standard programs to do word processing and financial calculations. These standard programs, if bought separately for a general purpose microcomputer, would cost as much as the entire Osborne 1 computer. The Osborne 1 uses the Z80 microprocessor and the CP/M operating system, but it has no bus, S-100 or otherwise. (See Figure 1-1.)

Mr. Fogarty was taken aback.

"What's the catch?" he asked. "This thing is half the price of a low-end, general purpose microcomputer, not counting all the free programs."

"If this microcomputer is adequate for your needs," Susan replied, "it's probably a good buy. But remember, it's an integrated microcomputer, which means that what you see is what you get. You can buy different printers for this microcomputer, or you can attach a larger monitor to it as an extra option, but you cannot exchange the floppy disk drives for bigger ones. If you discover that these floppy disk drives are not big enough for you, you have to get another machine."

"Maybe," Mr. Fogarty replied, "but from what I have seen around the stores a larger pair of floppy disk drives would cost as much as this whole microcomputer. Are there any other microcomputers like this one?"

"**Hewlett-Packard's HP-85A Desk-Top Computer** is an integrated microcomputer," Susan replied, "but it is very expensive, and it has tape cassettes instead of floppy disks."

Special Purpose Microcomputers

There are innumerable special purpose microcomputers manufactured today. We will summarize a few of the more popular types of special purpose microcomputers.

If you have a specialized application, find out if someone makes a product specifically for your needs before you look at general purpose microcomputers. You will probably pay a little more for this special product, but it will be worth the extra money.

Microcomputers for Computer Graphics

Computer graphics represent one of the most rapidly developing applications for microcomputers. If you are serious about using computer graphics you should use a color monitor as your display device. Inexpensive microcomputer systems use color television sets which are incapable of producing the quality of color and fine resolution which can be obtained by using inexpensive microcomputers.

RAMTEK   **Very good high quality color graphics systems are manufactured by RAMTEK Corporation.** These systems are not cheap, but they offer superb quality and versatility.

Compucolor   **Compucolor** sells microcomputer systems with color graphics that are almost as good as those of RAMTEK, but much less expensive. (See Figure 2-12.)

Cromemco   **Cromemco,** which we mentioned as being among the high-end, general purpose microcomputer manufacturers, also has an excellent

Photo courtesy of Compucolor Corp.

Figure 2-12. Compucolor microcomputer

product for those seeking color graphics with high resolution. Cromemco was the first company to offer an interface which allowed early microcomputer owners to use a color television set as their display.

Texas Instruments **The Texas Instruments 99/4 video games computer has color graphics that are among the best.** This is a low-end color graphics computer, but in comparison to other, more expensive products, it is very difficult to program.

Instrumentation and Control Microcomputers

Microcomputers are frequently used in industry to record data from various instruments and to control machinery of all types.

There are two important features that a microcomputer must have for instrumentation and control applications: the ability to transmit and receive analog signals and the presence of an IEEE 488 bus interface.

Analog and Digital Signals Analog signals are electrical signals which can change continuously. Digital signals can have one of two levels, and nothing in between. All standard microcomputers use digital logic, but you can buy additional components that let any general purpose microcomputer transmit and receive analog signals. If your purpose in buying a microcomputer is to transmit analog signals you would do well to first look at microcomputers that have been built specifically to process analog signals. (For more details see Chapter 6.)

IEEE 488   The IEEE 488 bus is a standard communications highway used by
Bus people who build instruments. If you are going to buy a microcomputer
to control these instruments or record their data, make sure it has an
IEEE 488 bus.

Suddenly, the Market Changed from A to Z

Soon after Mr. Fogarty purchased his microcomputer, the big three
microcomputer companies, already seriously challenged by low-priced
computers such as the Osborne 1, were facing competition with high-
priced computers manufactured by Xerox and IBM.

Xerox 820   **The Xerox 820 uses the standard CP/M operating system.** This
means that more than 2000 software packages are readily available for
implementation on the machine the day it was first delivered.

Although it can be used as a general purpose microcomputer, **the
primary application of the 820 is word processing.** It has a keyboard
with additional, special function keys to make this task simpler, and it
will readily interface to the Diablo 630 daisy wheel (letter quality)
printer. One of its special features is that it can be used as a typewriter to
type out labels, envelopes, short letters, and other jobs for which
memory storage is not required.

But in comparison to other microcomputers, **the 820 is not a cheap
system. After you buy the necessary software and an optional printer,
as well as the basic unit which includes dual 5-inch floppy drives, the
price is around $6000.** However, many large companies will buy 820's
by the dozens because they can lease them at low monthly rates and
because Xerox has a good reputation for backing up its products with
quality service. If you have a maintenance contract, when your 820
breaks down you can expect a Xerox technician to fix it within 24 hours.
This is a real selling point when you consider that most microcomputers
have to be returned to the stores where they were purchased or shipped
back to the manufacturer for repair, which can be a delay of a few days
or a few months.

The IBM Personal   From that moment back in 1975 when it became apparent that
Computer microcomputers were here to stay, rumors began to fly about the immi-
nent announcement of an IBM personal computer.

IBM has dominated the traditional computer market since the very
beginning. As one of the world's largest corporations, its identity is so
well known that to many people IBM and computers are synonymous.
How this giant could sit back and let companies like Radio Shack and

Apple rake in all the rewards of a lucrative new segment of the computer market was beyond belief.

Finally, on August 12, 1981, the speculation ceased. IBM unveiled its personal computer, which is simply called the IBM Personal Computer.

The basic IBM system, like the basic Apple II, has a keyboard which can be interfaced to a standard audio cassette player and a television set. Retailing for $1565, this system, which has superior color graphics, is adequate for video games and educational programs.

The IBM Personal Computer, interfaced to a single disk drive and a monochrome monitor, sells for around $3000. A complete system with dual drives and a printer can cost as much as $6000.

While the IBM machine is being initially offered with an operating system that is similar to, but not compatible with, CP/M, the company announced it would soon offer a genuine CP/M operating system as an option.

Like the Xerox 820, the IBM microcomputer has special function keys to make word processing easier. It is also backed by traditional IBM service.

The major difference between the IBM Personal Computer and all the others is that it has a 16-bit microprocessor instead of the standard 8-bit microprocessor. It can address up to 256K bytes of internal memory instead of 65K bytes, which is standard for 8-bit microprocessors. Thus, in the not too distant future, it will be possible to run longer and more sophisticated programs on the IBM microcomputer than are possible on 8-bit machines, but the extra memory will cost extra dollars.

What the Future Holds

By the time you read this, the microcomputer market will probably have gone through many new upheavals. For one thing, **several Japanese electronics companies have introduced powerful and elegant microcomputers that could have a major impact when they are marketed.**

Before you buy a microcomputer, you must know exactly what you want your microcomputer to do both now and in the future. Then shop for a machine which will accomplish the tasks you need. Do your homework and you won't fall into traps like those that befell our hapless Mr. Fogarty.

3
Software Makes Your
Microcomputer Go

A microcomputer without software is similar to a record player without records. Both are virtually worthless.

Some of the first microcomputer owners must have felt somewhat cheated. After spending days, weeks, or even months assembling their microcomputer kits they discovered there was little they could do other than turn them on and watch the front panel lights blink.

Actually, it wasn't quite that bleak. As we pointed out earlier, microcomputers differ from record players because you can program them yourself. With a microcomputer you can, in effect, make your own music.

Machine Language

Programming in machine language is akin to writing in Morse code. Instead of writing down words such as "Dear Mom and Dad," suppose you had to write down the series of dots and dashes representing each letter.

In machine language programming you communicate with the microcomputer using binary-number codes (1s and 0s). These codes were entered into the early microcomputers using a row of toggle switches, where up represented a "1" and down a "0."

The only practical aspect of the early machines was that all this fiddling with the toggle switches helped users learn about machine language programming and the internal architecture of the computer. Some hobbyists became engrossed with this, spending hours flipping switches; in at least one case, a hobbyist had to wear rubber gloves to keep his fingers from bleeding.

Why not just hook up the computer to a video terminal and typewriter keyboard and eliminate the toggle switch routine? That was definitely the manufacturer's intention, and eventually the microcomputer became the centerpiece of highly developed systems; but this step was a lot more complicated than simply plugging together components.

Device Drivers **The software programs needed for any microcomputer to communicate with external devices are called, appropriately enough, *device drivers*. These are small programs which have to be written for each device that is connected to the microcomputer.**

Unless you become an expert programmer, you will probably never write one of these programs. Today's microcomputers come with device drivers.

ROM Chip The first microcomputer device driver was called a *bootstrap loader*. It was written to interface a microcomputer to a teletype terminal. Initially, this device driver consisted of machine code printed or typed on paper. You had to physically enter it, line by line, using the front panel switches. Soon, though, it was made available in a small memory chip called a *ROM* (Read-Only Memory).

As its name implies, **a ROM is a memory chip whose contents you can read, but not write into. The contents of a ROM chip are fixed forever and can never be changed.**

ROM chips are important because they are used to permanently store programs inside the microcomputer.

RAM Chip **Programs not stored in internal memory are loaded from external memory into a different kind of memory chip called a *RAM* (Random Access Memory). RAM is memory that you can write into and read from.**

Monitor Device drivers are only the first of several "software building blocks" which form the basis for a truly powerful microcomputer system. **The next building block is the *monitor*.**

This software, which resides in ROM in most microcomputers, monitors the flow of data to and from the keyboard, directing it to the processor and the video screen, and controlling overall computer operations. In early microcomputers, the monitor was little more than a device driver to the keyboard. But **today's more sophisticated monitors handle a number of other interrelated tasks.**

Editor   **This brings us to the next building block, the *editor*. This program enables the entry and editing of programs.** The editor is a crude version of its more sophisticated cousin, word processing.

DOS   **Today the *Disk Operating System* (DOS) has become the most crucial microcomputer building block. This software controls the flow of data between the system's internal memory and external disks.**

Thanks to DOS software, the physical location of files on diskettes is invisible and, better still, unimportant to the user. Thus, loading a particular program or data file from a disk into a microcomputer's internal memory typically only requires that you enter the LOAD command followed by the correct file name. An example is

LOAD "Payroll"

Likewise, to save a program or file, you typically enter

SAVE "Payroll"

There are many DOS packages with varied capabilities available on different microcomputers.

CP/M   **The best known DOS package is part of an overall microcomputer control program known as CP/M.** This control program, sometimes called a ***Microcomputer Operating System,*** also includes an assembler, general purpose editor, and a sophisticated debugger.

The creation of microcomputer pioneer Gary Kildall, CP/M is by far **the most popular software package of its kind.** It is available on most 8080 and Z80 microprocessor-based microcomputers and will work with nearly any disk system. Because of this, many software companies (in addition to Kildall's own Digital Research) have developed both programming languages and application programs to run on CP/M. The library of CP/M programs is the largest software library available.

Many of today's popular microcomputers are CP/M-based machines. These include the Xerox 820, Hewlett-Packard 125, Osborne 1, Wangwriter, and most S-100 based microcomputers. The IBM Personal Computer comes with its own unique DOS, but a version of CP/M, CPM-86, is offered as an option. CP/M is available on the Apple II only with the addition of the Microsoft's Z-80 Softcard, a plug-in circuit board that converts the Apple from a 6502 microprocessor-based machine to a Z80-based machine.

Programming Language

Instead of being programmed in machine language, a microcomputer can be programmed in a *programming language* which is much simpler to understand.

Assembly   **Instead of assigning a binary number to each machine instruction,**
Language   ***assembly language* assigns each instruction a word or abbreviation.**
The resulting instruction name is called a *mnemonic*.

As in writing in machine code, **assembly language requires a detailed understanding of computers.** One problem is the tremendous discrepancy between the instructions recognized by a microcomputer and the tasks it is called upon to perform. Machine language instructions add the contents of two memory locations, move the contents from one location to another, or generate a new program address. On the other hand, you want a microcomputer to figure your payroll or issue checks. Translating the task you want performed into a sequence of assembly language instructions can be a very difficult process.

Furthermore, assembly languages differ from one another. **Assembly language programs are not portable.** An assembly language program written to perform a task on a microcomputer with an 8080 microprocessor chip is completely different from one written to perform the same task on a microcomputer with a 6502 microprocessor chip.

However, because assembly code has a one-to-one relationship with machine code (each instruction is an assigned mnemonic) **assembly language is often the most powerful way to program with a programming language.**

BASIC   **BASIC, an acronym for "Beginner's All-Purpose Symbolic Instruction Code," is by far the most popular microcomputer programming language.** Originally, it was created on minicomputers in the late 1960s by a Dartmouth professor, John Kemerry. Professor Kemerry was looking for a language that would make computers accessible to all students at Dartmouth, not just those in the computer science department.

One key to the success of Kemerry's language was that the new language was **based on familiar English language words.** The other key was that **BASIC was an interactive language.** Thus, as you entered and ran a BASIC program, the computer would react to it immediately. BASIC was quite unlike prevailing programming languages of the 1960s that forced you to create a program on computer cards and feed these cards into the computer.

Professor Kemerry's language was so popular that by 1970 virtually every student at Dartmouth had had some programming experience. It was used in other universities, and through commerical interests, BASIC was refined and improved for business use. Today many versions of BASIC are available.

BASIC is a general purpose language that is relatively easy to use. Unlike assembly language, there is no one-to-one relationship between a BASIC instruction and a machine language instruction. Instead, each BASIC instruction is equivalent to several machine language instructions. For this reason, while BASIC is easier to use, it doesn't have quite the speed of an assembly language.

The first microcomputer program using BASIC was written by Bill Gates and Paul Allen, who founded Microsoft, a major software company. Microsoft BASIC is standard software on nearly every major microcomputer. The other widely used BASIC is CBASIC, which runs on many CP/M-based microcomputers.

Learning to use BASIC on a microcomputer is an easy task; it does not require knowledge of computer science or advanced mathematics. There are dozens of tutorial books on how to use BASIC, as well as many classes in high schools, colleges, and community colleges.

Pascal   The second most popular microcomputer programming language is Pascal. Similar to BASIC because it uses standard English language commands called *key words,* Pascal is **said to be a better language than BASIC, because it forces you to adopt good programming practices**.

Pascal has fewer variations than BASIC; thus, programs written in Pascal and in particular *UCSD Pascal,* a version developed at the University of California at San Diego, can be run without much modification on different microcomputers.

The debate among software experts about which is the better language — Pascal, BASIC, or one of many other languages — is unending, esoteric, and probably irrelevant. If you are learning to program a microcomputer, you are likely to be programming in Pascal or BASIC. Other languages of which you might be aware include FORTRAN, FORTH, and LISP; however, these languages have been implemented on fewer systems.

Once you've learned one programming language it will be easier to learn a second language. The most difficult aspect of programming is the concept of programming, not the particular language.

Programming has been described both as a science and an art. Usually the best programmers are people adept at defining and solving problems.

Application Programs

By far the largest and most significant category of microcomputer software is *application programs.* **These can be simple programs that balance a checkbook or complex programs that manage the finances of a large business.**

Application programs can be written in assembly language or in one of the higher-level languages. In this chapter we will examine some of the more common application programs used on microcomputers.

Word Processing   **Microcomputers are widely used in word processing systems.**

A minimum requirement for word processing is an 80-column screen with which you can display and subsequently print out 80 characters per line. Obviously, a machine that will generate only upper-case characters is inadequate.

There are dozens of word processing software packages designed for use on microcomputers. This creates problems because no two packages are the same. Some of them are quite sophisticated while others are extremely simple.

Wordwrap   One way to spot an inferior word processing software package is to find out if it has *wordwrap.* **This feature automatically moves a word which does not fit at the end of the line being typed to the next line.** It is almost always combined with an automatic carriage return. Together these two features allow you to enter text into your word processor in a continuous stream of typing.

Some of the more ridiculous word processing software has an automatic carriage return feature without wordwrap. Thus, the last word on a line is often divided between that line and the next, as shown below:

As you can see in this example, it is somew
hat difficult to read text on a screen wi
thout wordwrap. If a word does not fit o
n a line it is simply continued on the foll
owing line.

In addition to wordwrap, **a good word processor should make editing easy**. In other words, you should be able to insert or delete characters, words, or lines of text without problems. On most good systems you insert words or text by moving the cursor to the desired location and then typing the corrections. To delete you should be able to place the cursor next to the desired character, word, or line and then press one or two keys. Less sophisticated systems do not let you edit while creating a document. Thus, before you are able to edit, you have to press a series of keys putting you in "edit mode." Then, after you have edited, you must return to "create mode" to enter more text.

Mail Merge

The most widely used microcomputer word processing software is WordStar, a package developed and sold by MicroPro. This software runs on any microcomputer with CP/M and 50K bytes of RAM. **It has many advanced features including subscript, superscript, automatic page numbering, and footing and heading codes**. With WordStar you can edit one document while printing another.

Before buying a word processor you should investigate the available products.

There is more to word processing than merely typing documents. Many word processing packages come with additional capabilities or additional software packages that can be used in tandem with the basic software.

The most common word processing supplement is *mail merge*. With this feature you can merge a list of names, addresses, or variable information with a form letter to create personalized "computer" letters. Depending upon the software you have, the variables can be any word or phrase in the document which you want to vary from one letter to the next. For example, suppose you were using mail merge to send out thank-you letters to people who donated to a fund-raising campaign. One of the variables might be the amount of each contributor's donation, as shown in the following example:

John Brown
816 Forbes Road
Wishingwell, Wisconsin

Dear John,
Thank you very much for your donation of $20 for the save the fruit fly fund. With your help and that of thousands like you we are making headway in our struggle to save this endangered species.

Sincerely,
Arnold Grossberger
Committee Chairman

Annette Rowbarth
942 Overdrive Road
Alliance, Ohio

Dear Annette,

Thank you very much for your donation of $85 for the save the fruit fly fund. With your help and that of thousands like you we are making headway in our struggle to save this endangered species.

Sincerely,

Arnold Grossberger
Committee Chairman

Because of the widespread use of microcomputers, the ability to create personalized computer letters is no longer exclusive to large organizations which can afford large computer systems. This one use alone justifies the purchase of microcomputer systems in many small businesses.

List Processing Sophisticated mail merge or *list processing* programs can be used to maintain long lists of names, addresses, and any related information such as products purchased by individual customers. Furthermore, these programs allow for lists to be accessed selectively. In this way, they can send letters or forms to all the customers in a particular ZIP code area or to all customers who have purchased a particular product.

Electronic Dictionaries **Electronic spelling dictionaries that correct common misspellings are another aid to word processing equipment.** These programs store 15,000 to 25,000 standard words with the capacity to add several thousand additional words to suit individual needs. They work by scanning every word in a document and stopping at any word which doesn't match up with a word in the dictionary. Some of them automatically display alternatives and allow you to select the correct word with a keystroke. Others require that you enter your own corrections.

Other auxiliary word processing programs include electronic indexing, automatic page numbering, footnotes, addressing envelopes, and much more.

Electronic Spread Sheets **Another major area of microcomputer applications is electronic spread sheets. This software is used as a business analysis tool for creating projection charts such as cash flow analysis, sales projections, revenue projections, and cost estimates.** Almost any task traditionally performed with a calculator or adding machine, pencil, or graph paper can be done with this software.

The advantage of electronic spread sheets over traditional methods is their automatic calculating and recalculating features. As you enter figures into a chart, results affected by your entries (such as totals, averages, projections, and so forth) are instantly calculated.

VisiCalc, from VisiCorp, was the first software package of this type to be used on microcomputers. Originally written to run on the Apple II, it has since been translated to many other machines, including the IBM Personal Computer. There are many other electronic spread sheets available, including SuperCalc and T/Maker, which have enhanced editing features. SuperCalc and T/Maker work on any CP/M-based system.

Data Base Management

A data base is a computerized filing cabinet full of information with a superior indexing system. With this software you can create your own data base and store any type of information you may subsequently want to retrieve.

Data base software gives you two advantages over manual filing. The first is speed of access and the second is the ability to automatically produce reports. For example, if your company maintains a customer data base, you may want to write a report showing such things as geographic dispersal, the percentage of customers who have ordered particular products, the number of repeat customers, and so forth.

Unfortunately, many of the microcomputer data base programs offered today are poor. They are thinly disguised modifications of the programming tools provided by an operating system. Very few have been designed for nontechnical users, but a few data base programs are very good.

Some data base programs are designed to link various pieces of information. You provide the data base with a few key words or phrases and the data base program builds a picture of all information in the data base that relates to the words or phrases you have provided. Other data base programs let you prepare reports. These programs allow you to define the format of the report and specify the columns of numbers which the program will fetch from the data base. All this is printed to your specifications.

When looking at any data base program, you should expect and demand that the program make sense to you, even if you know little about computers or programming.

Accounting Programs

Accounting programs include payroll, accounts payable, accounts receivable, general ledger, and inventory features.

There are two important features to look for in accounting programs: modularity and interaction. Modular programs can be used individually or in combination.

Interactive programs automatically feed information from one module to another so that you don't enter the same information twice. For example, payroll, accounts payable, and accounts receivable modules may all feed information directly to a general ledger. However, when any one of these modules is absent, it should be possible to enter the absent module's information by hand. Small businesses frequently run a general ledger module without any other accounting system components.

Payroll occasionally includes labor cost distribution. This option, if available, is only useful on microcomputer systems with a million or more bytes of diskette or disk storage capacity. Without this option, payroll is the least useful accounting program since banks and data processing services provide very inexpensive payroll processing.

There are two separate and distinct types of inventory: order entry inventory and manufacturing inventory. Order entry inventory is geared to sales. As products are ordered and sold, they are deleted from inventory. Reports are produced which tell you which products are selling the fastest and when to reorder or restock individual items. Some order entry programs automatically order new items either by automatically filling out order forms or by sending requests via a data communication line to a computer at a distribution center.

Fun and Games   **Perhaps the most publicized use of microcomputers is for fun and games.** There are thousands of game programs for microcomputers, ranging from paddle games to space war games to sophisticated fantasy games.

Many computer games are based on *simulation science.* This is a subset of the kind of programming in which computers simulate flying conditions for pilot training. This programming may also be used to design games such as "Lunar Lander™," where the object is to safely land a spacecraft on the moon by controlling such variables as fuel consumption.

If you want to play games on a microcomputer you'll probably want one that has color graphics and sound. The ATARI 400 and 800 microcomputers are two of the most popular game-playing microcomputers because they have graphics and sound.

As the microcomputer market grows, the need to know programming in order to make use of a microcomputer diminishes. Radio Shack, for instance, has published two volumes of a book called *TRS-80 Applications Software Sourcebook,* which lists more than 2000 programs you can buy for the TRS-80. These include hundreds of business accounting programs, education programs, home programs, game programs, and programs specific to an industry or profession.

Although they are still in development, there are even programs that program! These software packages, if they ever live up to the expectations of their designers, could forever eliminate the need to program.

In the meantime, however, even though many thousands of programs have been written, there are millions of potential applications waiting to be implemented on microcomputers.

If you are interested in how microcomputers work, we suggest you read Section II of this book and then the second book in this series, *An Introduction to Microcomputers: Volume 1*. However, if you can't wait to get your hands on a system to use for an existing application, or to learn how to program in a higher-level language such as Pascal or BASIC, we suggest you read the *Business System Buyer's Guide* (Osborne and Cook, Osborne/McGraw-Hill, 1981) to give you additional insights into what system to buy. There are many fine tutorials on programming in higher-level languages available from both computer manufacturers and publishers. See your local computer dealer for details.

4

Getting Down to Basics

We are now going to look inside a microcomputer and see how it works.

Levels of Knowledge

You can buy a microcomputer system and use it as such, writing programs in a programming language (such as FORTRAN or BASIC). If that is what you plan to do, then you don't need to know how the microcomputer system works, and the rest of this book will be of little value to you. Read the first few pages of Chapter 5, which discusses programming languages, then find a book that teaches you the programming language in which you plan to work.

But programming a microcomputer system using a language such as FORTRAN or BASIC is like taking the bus. In order to ride on a bus, you don't need to know how a bus works or even how to drive one. However, if you want the flexibility of a private car, you must learn to drive. In order to repair your car you have to learn how it works. Similarly, **if you want to access the power and capabilities of your microcomputer — rather than accessing the lesser power and more limited capabilities of a programming language — then you must learn how the microcomputer works.**

If you decide to learn how a microcomputer works, you need to identify the level of knowledge you seek. You can learn how to program the microcomputer using a very fundamental, microcomputer-level programming language, or you can go a step further and learn enough about how the microcomputer works to repair it if it fails — and to expand or change it if it doesn't meet your needs.

In the following chapters we will explain some very fundamental concepts, aimed at bringing you to the point where you can understand *An Introduction to Microcomputers: Volume 1 — Basic Concepts.* **If you want to do more than program a microcomputer using a higher-level language, you must read the rest of this book. Only when you read subsequent books in the series will you start discriminating between information you need or do not need, depending on your aspirations.**

While discussing fundamental concepts, we will continuously refer to the microcomputer itself, but not to the physical units surrounding it. It will be a long time, if ever, before you need more information on floppy disks, keyboards, displays and other physical units, or their interface logic. You will buy the physical unit and its interface logic as a single unit, and you will program the physical unit from the microcomputer.

Numbers and Logic

Every piece of logic within a microcomputer system may be reduced to a network of switches, each of which is "on" or "off." This is a concept that is not entirely new to you, since we used it to describe memories, and specifically, read-only memories. But, **let us look at how a network of switches can ultimately generate the power and versatility of a computer.**

Binary Data

Consider numbers. As we have often stated, instructions, programs, and data of all kinds become a sequence of numbers. **How are we going to represent so many numbers, given nothing more than switches that may be on or off?**

The digit 0 can be represented by an off switch:

The digit 1 can represent an on switch:

Now what? A computer that can only count to 1 will not be very useful. **Computers can create only two separate and distinct numeric digits.**

Zero	0
One	1
Then what?	

But humans have a similar problem. We are limited to ten separate and distinct numeric digits.

Zero	0
One	1
Two	2
Three	3
Four	4
Five	5
Six	6
Seven	7
Eight	8
Nine	9
Now start combining digits!	
Ten	10
Eleven	11
etc.	

Decimal Numbers

The human number system is referred to as the decimal number system. The decimal number system appears worldwide, among unrelated tribes and nations — wherever societies have learned to count. This is probably because humans originally learned to count on their fingers. There is nothing "unique" or "natural" about the decimal counting system; in fact, it is a rather clumsy way of doing things. We will see later that there are much better ways of counting.

The Binary Number System

The computer counting system is referred to as the *binary system*. It has only two separate, distinct digits: 0 and 1. To represent numbers greater than 1 we follow the example of decimal numbers and use

more than one digit. Consider **the number 2;** in binary format it **is represented by the digits 10:**

Decimal		Binary	
Zero	0	Zero	0
One	1	One	1
Two	2	Two	10
Three	3		
Four	4		
Five	5		
Six	6		
Seven	7		
Eight	8		
Nine	9		
Ten	10		

In both the decimal and binary counting systems the two-digit combination 10 represents a number that is one greater than the largest single-digit number. In the decimal number system, the largest single-digit number is 9; therefore, 10 represents one more than 9. In the binary number system, the largest single-digit number is 1; therefore, 10 represents one more than 1, which is 2.

The numeric value of the digit combination 10 is very important. This digit combination has the value ten in the decimal system, which is where the decimal system gets its name. Similarly, in the binary system, the digit combination 10 has the value two, which is where the word *binary* comes from.

Number Base   **These values, ten for the decimal system and two for the binary system, are called the *base* for the numeric system.**

The base number (that is, the value associated with the digit combination 10) is interpreted for decimal or binary numbers as follows:

Ones Digit   The digits of a two-digit decimal number are referred to as the *ones* **Tens Digit**   digit and the *tens* digit:

Twos Digit   For a two-digit binary number, the digits are referred to as the *ones* digit and the *twos* digit.

To represent three using binary numbers, we can still draw a parallel with our decimal counting system. **The next decimal number after decimal 10 is created by adding 1 as follows:**

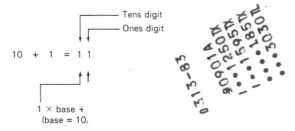

Similarly, we advance from 2 to 3 ⟶ ...ry numbers by adding 1 to binary 2.

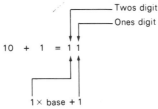

What happens when we want to create 4 using binary numbers? The parallel with decimal counting is not immediately visible. Following decimal 11, we still have a long way to go before problems arise. We can keep on adding 1 until we reach decimal 19.

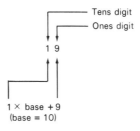

Then we go to decimal 20.

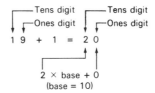

It is not until you reach decimal 99 that you have to add a third decimal digit and create 100.

In the binary system, following binary 11 (which is decimal 3), we have a problem. If we add 1 to 11 we cannot get 12, because the digit 2 does not exist in the binary system. Morever, we cannot go from 11 to 20, because once again we are using 2, which is an illegal binary digit. **Binary numbers** must, therefore, follow **11 with 100.**

Zero	0
One	1
Two	10
Three	11
Four	100

Let us examine the meaning of three-digit numbers.

When you see the number 234, you automatically interpret it as two hundred and thirty-four.

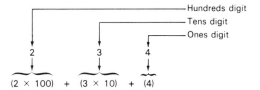

Hundreds Digit

But there is a special significance to the *hundreds* digit, just as there is to the *tens* digit. You can increment the tens digit nine times; on the tenth increment you must increment the hundreds digit. Consider tens digit increments, beginning with the decimal number 3.

			3	Three
First increment		1	3	Thirteen
Second increment		2	3	Twenty-three
Third increment		3	3	Thirty-three
Fourth increment		4	3	Forty-three
Fifth increment		5	3	Fifty-three
Sixth increment		6	3	Sixty-three
Seventh increment		7	3	Seventy-three
Eighth increment		8	3	Eighty-three
Ninth increment		9	3	Ninety-three
Tenth increment!!	1	0	3	One hundred three

Fours   In the case of binary numbers, you can increment the *twos* digit just
Digit   once; on the second increment, you must create a *fours* digit.

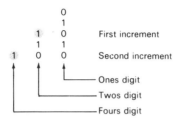

Here is the rule: the number of times you can increment a digit is
equal to one less than the number base, after which you must increment the next higher digit. Thus, in a decimal number you can increment any digit nine times (0 to 9), at which point you must increment
the next higher decimal digit. In a binary number, you can increment
once (0 to 1) before incrementing the next higher binary digit. Thus,
digits can be represented as follows:

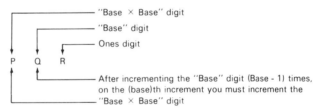

In the illustration above, P, Q, and R represent any number system's
digits. Substitute 2 or 10 for *base* and the illustration will represent
"binary" or "decimal" numbers.

The second digit of a multidigit number becomes a *number base*
multiplier within an equation that tells you the value of the multidigit
numbers. Similarly, a third digit becomes a multiplier for the number
base multiplied by itself. This may be illustrated as follows:

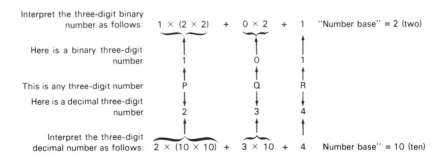

Square of a Number

A number multiplied by itself is referred to as the *square* of the number. Thus **we can represent any three-digit number by the following general-purpose equation:**

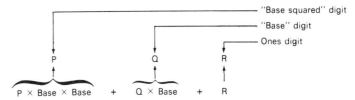

For "Base × Base" we use the symbol Base^2. Thus Base^2 represents the square of the number represented by Base.

We can extend the same reasoning to larger numbers.

Thousands Digit

Cube of a Number

In decimal arithmetic, a fourth digit identifies thousands, and is referred to as the *thousands* digit. For example, 2345 represents two thousand, three hundred forty-five. A thousand is $10 \times 10 \times 10$, which is the same thing as "number base" × "number base" × "number base"; this is the *cube* of the number base. For "Base × Base × Base" we use the symbol Base^3. Thus, Base^3 represents the cube of the number represented by "Base."

Eights Digit

A four-digit binary number will be interpreted as follows:

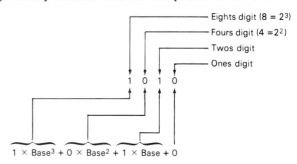

We can now define multidigit decimal and binary numbers as follows:

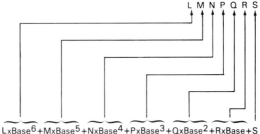

The general definition just shown is for a seven-digit number; any other number of digits could be represented by adding digits at the left end of the number.

Each time you multiply Base^n by Base you get Base^{n+1}. Thus Base through Base^6 have the following values:

	Binary		Decimal
Two	Base		Ten
Four	Base^2		One Hundred
Eight	Base^3		One Thousand
Sixteen	Base^4		Ten Thousand
Thirty-two	Base^5		One hundred thousand
Sixty-four	Base^6		One million

High-Order Digit

Low-Order Digit

In any multidigit number we refer to the ones digit — the rightmost digit — as the *low-order* digit. The leftmost digit is called the *high-order* digit. This may be illustrated as follows:

Binary-to-Decimal Conversion

You can use the general representation of a multidigit number to convert any binary number to its decimal equivalent.

The following are some examples of multidigit binary numbers, showing how to figure out their decimal equivalents:

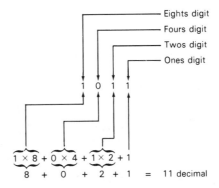

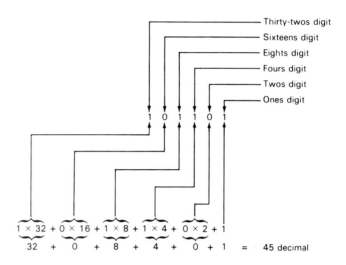

Decimal-to-Binary Conversion

There is a very simple technique for converting any decimal number to its binary equivalent; we will define this technique, then explain why it works.

Here is a definition of the technique: to convert a decimal number to its binary equivalent, divide the decimal number by 2 repeatedly until nothing is left of the number. The following are two examples:

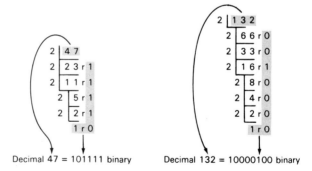

Decimal 47 = 101111 binary   Decimal 132 = 10000100 binary

Now we will explain why the conversion technique works.

The steps illustrated above create the multidigit binary equivalent of the decimal number; the least significant (that is, the rightmost) binary digit is created first. This digit is the remainder, once you know how many twos digits there are.

Let us use the symbol NNN to represent any decimal number. What happens when we divide NNN by 2? We will get half of NNN, plus a remainder of 0 or 1. Let us use the symbol PPP to represent half of NNN. In the general case, we illustrate NNN being divided by 2 by the following:

```
2 | NNN
    PPP    remainder   0 or 1
```

The following are some specific cases:

```
2 | 421                  (NNN = 421)
    210    remainder 1   (PPP = 210)


2 | 36                   (NNN = 36)
    18     remainder 0   (PPP = 18)


2 | 7                    (NNN = 7)
    3      remainder 1   (PPP = 3)
```

In each of the above illustrations the decimal number NNN is shown as having PPP twos digits, plus 0 or 1.

```
NNN =  PPP  ×  2  +  remainder
421 =  210  ×  2  +  1
 36 =   18  ×  2  +  0
  7 =    3  ×  2  +  1
```

For any decimal number NNN, in order to discover how many twos digits there are (PPP), you simply divide the decimal number (NNN) by 2. The remainder (0 or 1) is the ones digit.

What about PPP? It is a decimal number. If by chance PPP is 0 or 1, then it is also a valid binary number; any larger number is not a valid binary number. If the number of twos digits computed in the first step above (PPP) is more than 1, that means fours digits are in the binary number. In order to calculate how many fours digits there are, you could simply divide the initial decimal number by 4.

```
4 | NNN
    QQQ    remainder 3, 2, 1 or 0
```

Look again at our previous examples.

```
NNN =  QQQ  ×  4  +  remainder
421 =  105  ×  4  +  1
 36 =    9  ×  4  +  0
  7 =    1  ×  4  +  3
```

But note that QQQ, the number of fours digits, must be half of PPP, the number of twos digits; that is to say, dividing NNN by 4 is the same as dividing half of NNN by 2:

```
4 | NNN                    is the same as    2 | NNN
     QQQ   remainder 3, 2, 1 or 0              2 | PPP   remainder 1 or 0
                                                   QQQ   remainder 1 or 0


4 | 421                    is the same as    2 | 421
     105   remainder 1                         2 | 210   remainder 1
                                                   105   remainder 0


4 | 36                     is the same as    2 | 36
     9   remainder 0                          2 | 18   remainder 0
                                                  9   remainder 0


4 | 7                      is the same as    2 | 7
     1   remainder 3                          2 | 3   remainder 1
                                                  1   remainder 1
```

The advantage of dividing by 2 twice is that all remainders are 0 or 1 — valid binary digits. Look at those remainders illustrated above.

```
1   is the same as   01   (binary)
0   is the same as   00   (binary)
3   is the same as   11   (binary)
```

Decimal 7 (7_{10}) has become binary 111 (111_2). That is, decimal 7 equals one fours digit, plus one twos digit, plus one ones digit:

$$7_{10} = 4_{10} + 2_{10} + 1_{10}$$

Decimal numbers 36_{10} and 421_{10} must continue to have higher-level binary digits created since 9_{10} and 105_{10} are not valid binary digits. Higher-level binary digits are created by continuing to divide by 2. The following is the complete conversion for 36:

```
2 | 3 6
  2 | 1 8   remainder 0 (no ones digits)
    2 | 9   remainder 0 (no twos digits)
      2 | 4   remainder 1 (one fours digit)
        2 | 2   remainder 0 (no eights digits)
            1   remainder 0 (no sixteens digits)
            ↑
        one thirty-twos digit
```

Thus,

$$36_{10} = 32_{10} + 4_{10} = 100100_2$$

Decimal Notation In the illustration above, we have introduced a new form of shorthand which is commonly used in computer books. **Decimal numbers are identified by a 10 subscript at the end of the number.**

Decimal 4713 is represented as 4713_{10}

Binary Notation **Binary numbers are identified by a 2 subscript at the end of the number.**

Binary 11010 is represented as 11010_2

Since you are repeatedly dividing the decimal number by 2, the remainder can only be 0 or 1 — and the remainder tells you how many ones digits, twos digits, fours digits, and so on, there are in the binary equivalent of the decimal number. If QQQ is 2 or more, there are more than 0 or 1 fours digits, and you divide the fours digits (QQQ) by two to determine how many eights digits there are. The remainder, when you divide the fours digits (QQQ) by two, tells you whether there are 0 or 1 fours digits. If there is more than one eights digit, you go on to the sixteens digits; and if there is more than one sixteens digit you go on to the thirty-twos digits; and so on.

Table 4-1 summarizes all possible four-digit binary numbers and gives their decimal equivalents.

As you look at Table 4-1, it is easy to see how switches can be used to represent numbers of any size. A 0 becomes an off switch while a 1 becomes an on switch. By simply increasing the number of switches used to represent a number, you can indefinitely increase the size of the numbers that switches can represent. **Table 4-2 shows you the largest number that you can represent in the binary counting system as you increase the number of digits in the number.**

Notice that each time you add a new switch (or binary digit) you double the maximum number size which can be represented.

Bits, Nibbles, and Bytes

Bit **A binary digit is always referred to as a *bit*.** Thus, a bit can have a value of 0 or 1.

Byte Although numbers can be created from any number of binary digits, or bits, as illustrated in Table 4-2, there are certain numbers of bits

Table 4-1. All Four-Digit Binary Numbers and
Their Decimal Representations

Decimal Numbers	Binary Numbers
0	0000
1	0001
2	0010
3	0011
4	0100
5	0101
6	0110
6	0111
8	1000
9	1001
10	1010
11	1011
12	1100
13	1101
14	1110
15	1111

Table 4-2. The Largest Number that can be Represented by Binary
Numbers with 1 through 16 Digits

Number of Binary Digits	Maximum Binary Value	Decimal Equivalent
1	1	1
2	11	3
3	111	7
4	1111	15
5	11111	31
6	111111	63
7	1111111	127
8	11111111	255
9	111111111	511
10	1111111111	1023
11	11111111111	2047
12	111111111111	4095
13	1111111111111	8191
14	11111111111111	16383
15	111111111111111	32767
16	1111111111111111	65535

which you will frequently encounter. Most frequently you will deal with
8-bit combinations. **An 8-bit unit is referred to as a *byte*.** There are a
few obscure computers that use the word "byte" to describe some
other number of bits (most frequently 6 bits), but in the world of
microcomputers, the byte is always an 8-bit unit. Thus a byte can represent numbers in the range 0 through 255.

Nibble   **Units of four bits are sometimes referred to as *nibbles.* Thus, a byte** consists of two nibbles.

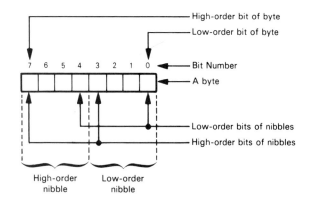

Word   **Units of 16 bits are sometimes called *words.* Thus, a word consists** of two bytes or four nibbles.

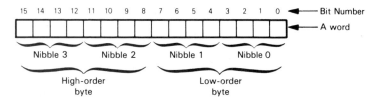

Binary Arithmetic

Let us look at parallels between **arithmetic using binary numbers** and arithmetic using decimal numbers.

Binary Addition

When you perform decimal addition, you align the digits of the two numbers being added as follows:

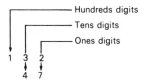

You do essentially the same thing for binary addition.

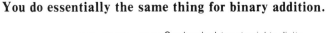

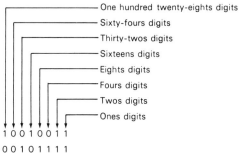

You add the numbers, one digit at a time, starting with the low-order (ones) digit. But binary addition is beautifully simple, compared to decimal addition. When you add two binary digits, there are just the four following possibilities:

$$
\begin{array}{cccc}
 & & & 1 \longleftarrow \text{Carry 1} \\
0 & 0 & 1 & 1 \\
\underline{+0} & \underline{+1} & \underline{+0} & \underline{+1} \\
0 & 1 & 1 & 0
\end{array}
$$

When you have two decimal digits, you have 100 possibilities, 45 of which will generate a carry.

Let us look at a few examples of binary addition, first the very simple 2+2=4. Using binary numbers, you get the following:

Decimal	Binary
0	000
1	001
2	010
3	011
4	100

Decimal	Binary
2	010
+ 2	+ 010
4	100

Here is a digit-by-digit explanation of the binary addition.

• The ones digits are both 0; adding them creates 0 and no carry.

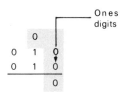

· The twos digits are both 1 and there is no carry from the ones digit. Adding the two 1 bits creates 0 plus a carry.

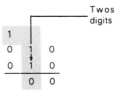

· The focus digits are both 0, but there is a carry from the twos digits. The two zeros create 0, but adding 1 (the carry) to 0 creates 1, with no carry.

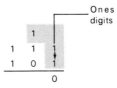

Now let us look at a slightly more complex example of binary addition: $7+5=12$. This may be illustrated as follows:

Decimal	Binary
7	111
+ 5	+ 101
12	1100

The ones digits are both 1; they sum to 0 and create a carry.

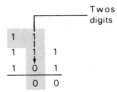

The twos digits are 1 and 0; there is also a carry from the ones digit. This is equivalent to adding the three bits: 1, 1, and 0, which creates 0 and a carry.

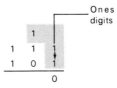

The fours digits are both 1, but there is also a carry from the twos digits. Adding three 1 bits is simple enough if you do it in two steps. First add two 1 bits.

$$\begin{array}{r} 1 \\ 1 \\ \hline 10 \end{array}$$

This creates 0 and a carry. Now add the third 1 bit to the result.

$$\begin{array}{r} 10 \\ 1 \\ \hline 11 \end{array}$$

You have 1 with a carry.

The eights digits are both 0, but there is a carry. The eights digits, therefore, sum to 1.

```
                                          Eights
                                          digits
     1   1   1
         1   1   1
         1   0   1
     ─────────────
     1   1   0   0
```

The addition of 132 and 47, which we illustrated earlier when describing microcomputer logic, in binary becomes

Decimal	Binary
132	10000100
+ 47	00101111
179	10110011

The decimal-to-binary conversions for 132 and 47 have already been described. **We can check that the binary sum is indeed equivalent to decimal 179 as follows:**

```
1 0 1 1 0 0 1 1

          1  ×    1  =     1
          1  ×    2  =     2
          0  ×    4  =     0
          0  ×    8  =     0
          1  ×   16  =    16
          1  ×   32  =    32
          0  ×   64  =     0
          1  ×  128  =   128
                       ───────
                          179
```

If you do not understand binary addition at this point, you should continue doing examples until this becomes clear. For each example, write two decimal numbers, then create their binary equivalents. Add the binary equivalents, and convert the sum back to a decimal value. If you do not get the correct decimal sum, you have made an error.

Binary Subtraction and Negative Numbers

Binary subtraction is far simpler than decimal subtraction because you have just four possibilities.
You may subtract 0 from 0 which leaves 0.

$$\begin{array}{r} 0 \\ -\ 0 \\ \hline 0 \end{array}$$

You may subtract 1 from 1 which again leaves 0.

$$\begin{array}{r} 1 \\ -\ 1 \\ \hline 0 \end{array}$$

If you subtract 0 from 1 the result is 1.

$$\begin{array}{r} 1 \\ -\ 0 \\ \hline 1 \end{array}$$

But what happens when you subtract 1 from 0? As in decimal subtraction, binary subtraction requires that you borrow from the next highest bit, as follows:

$$\begin{array}{r} \text{Borrowed} \\ 10 \\ -\ 1 \\ \hline 1 \end{array}$$

The binary representation of 2 is 10; the illustration above subtracts 1 from 2, leaving a result of 1. If there is no higher bit to borrow from, then the result is -1.

$$\begin{array}{r} 0 \\ -\ 1 \\ \hline -1 \end{array}$$

Extending subtraction to multibit (multiple binary digit) numbers is as simple as extending subtraction to multiple decimal digit numbers. The following is the binary equivalent of $4 - 2 = 2$:

$$\begin{array}{r} 100 \\ -\ 010 \\ \hline 010 \end{array}$$

Subtrahend   When you subtract two numbers, you subtract a *subtrahend* from a

Minuend   *minuend.* This may be illustrated as follows:

```
        4 ◄──────── Minuend
      – 2 ◄──────── Subtrahend
        2 ◄──────── Difference
```

Looking at the binary subtraction of 2 from 4, the ones digits are
both 0, and therefore the difference is 0.

```
                          ┌────────Ones digits
                          │
      1    0    0 ◄──────Minuend
      0    1    0 ◄──────Subtrahend
      ────────────
               0
```

In the case of the twos digits, we must subtract 1 from 0. Therefore,
we borrow 1 from the minuend fours digit and obtain a difference of 1.

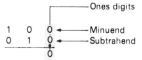

```
                              ┌──────────Twos digits
                              │
   1   0   0 }        { 0   10   0
   0   1   0 }───────►{ 0    1   0
                        ────────────
                             1    0
```

The minuend fours digit is now 0; the 1 that was there has been borrowed by the minuend twos digit. Thus, for the fours digits we subtract
0 from 0, creating a difference of 0.

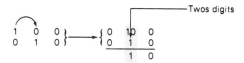

```
                    ┌──────────Fours digits
                    │
      0   10   0
      0    1   0
      ───────────
      0    1   0
```

**Going to a more complex example, the following is the binary
representation of $132_{10} - 47_{10} = 85_{10}$:**

Decimal	Binary
11	111 ◄────────Borrows
132	10000100 ◄────────Minuend
– 47	– 00101111 ◄────────Subtrahend
85	01010101 ◄────────Difference

The following is a step-by-step illustration of the binary subtraction:

```
1  0  0  0  0  1  0  0 ───────▶  1  0  0  0  0  0  1  10
0  0  1  0  1  1  1  1           0  0  1  0  1  1  1   1
                                                       1

1  0  0  0  0  0  1  1 ◀─        0  1  1  1  1  10  1  10
0  0  1  0  1  1  1  1           0  0  1  0  1   1  1   1
                     0  1                        1  0   1

0  1  1  1  1  10  1  10 ◀─
0  0  1  0  1   1  1   1
0  1  0  1  0   1  0   1
```

We can check that the binary result is correct by generating its decimal equivalent.

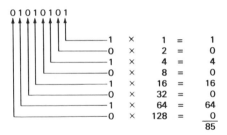

```
0 1 0 1 0 1 0 1

          1  ×   1   =    1
          0  ×   2   =    0
          1  ×   4   =    4
          0  ×   8   =    0
          1  ×  16   =   16
          0  ×  32   =    0
          1  ×  64   =   64
          0  × 128   =    0
                        ────
                          85
```

Now this may surprise you, but most computers cannot subtract. They can only add. Fortunately, this is no problem. Subtracting one number from another is equivalent to adding the negative of the number. This can be illustrated as follows:

$$4 + (-2) = +2$$

The above solution might look ridiculous, but, in fact it is not. It only looks ridiculous because you are used to decimal numbers. Consider the subtraction of 3 from 9. You could write this as $9-3$, or you could write it as $9+(0-3)$. In fact $9+(0-3)$ is more complicated than $9-3$. To solve $9+(0-3)$ you must subtract 3 from 0 before adding the result to 9; but when you subtract 3 from 0 you get -3, which puts you right back to subtracting 3 from 9, which was what you were going to do in the first place.

Subtraction in the world of switches and binary numbers cannot be resolved until we find a way of representing negative numbers. A switch is a two-state device and we cannot simply add a new state for the switch to represent a negative sign.

0   1   −

Until we find some means of representing negative binary numbers, we cannot even try to come up with the binary equivalent of $9 + (0 - 3)$.

In order to find some method of representing negative binary numbers, let's begin with the simple case of numbers in the range 0 through −7. In their positive form, these numbers are represented by three binary digits as follows:

Decimal	Binary Equivalent
0	000
1	001
2	010
3	011
4	100
5	101
6	110
7	111

We cannot arbitrarily select a method of representing negative binary numbers. Our requirement is that we be able to subtract by adding the negative representation of the number.

The logical way of finding a binary representation for negative numbers is to try subtracting the positive number from 0. Consider $+3$. Its binary form is 11_2. Let us see what happens when we subtract 11_2 from 00.

```
1 0 0 ◄──────Minuend
 − 1 1 ◄──────Subtrahend
 ─────
    ?
```

Starting with the ones digits, we want to subtract 1 from 0; that's impossible, so we try to borrow 1 from the minuend twos digit — which is also 0. If we assume that we can borrow 1 from the minuend fours digit (to the left of the twos digit), we get the following:

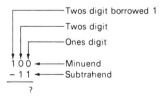

Now the minuend ones digit can borrow 1 from the minuend twos digit.

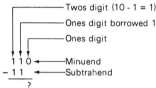

We can successfully perform the subtraction.

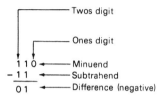

The difference in the ones digit is computed as $10_2 - 1_2 = 1_2$. This is equivalent to the decimal $2_{10} - 1_{10} = 1_{10}$.

The difference in the twos digit is simply $1 - 1 = 0$.

We have succeeded in subtracting 3 from 0 using binary arithmetic, but it involved a sleight-of-hand for which we must now account; we borrowed 1 from the next high-order digit of the minuend (the fours digit in this case) when no such digit existed.

We have another problem that now needs resolution. The two bits 01 are shown representing the value -3; but they also represent the value $+1$.

These two problems have no solution within the context of binary counting as we have defined it thus far. **In order to handle subtraction — and the inevitable negative numbers that can result — we must modify the rules adopted thus far for binary counting.** But the new set of rules must be logically and numerically consistent with the needs of positive binary numbers and the needs of binary arithmetic.

Fortunately, there is a simple solution. Let us look at a few signed decimal numbers.

+10	+123	+47	+83742
−10	−123	−47	−83742

The one new feature introduced by the numbers illustrated above is the sign; there is a plus sign $(+)$ and a minus sign $(-)$. Binary signed numbers could be illustrated as follows:

+1011	+1110101	+110	+1011010
−1011	−1110101	−110	−1011010

Sign of Binary Numbers   What we have is a plus (+) or minus (−) sign preceding the string of bits (binary digits). We cannot represent plus and minus signs as separate and distinct entities within computer logic. Remember, computer logic consists of nothing other than two-state switches. We must, therefore, take the same two-state switch which represents 0 and 1 digits, but now use it to represent plus and minus signs. If **we use an off switch to represent a plus sign, and an on switch to represent a minus sign,** then the plus sign (+) and the zero digit (0) are both represented by an off switch while the minus sign (−) and the one digit (1) are both represented by an on switch. Now **our signed binary numbers could be represented as follows:**

01011	01110101	0110	01011010	Positive numbers
11011	11110101	1110	11011010	Negative numbers

Unfortunately, the method of representing negative numbers illustrated above is not going to work. Consider the simple example of $5 - 3 = 2$. Remember, we said that in order to subtract we must be able to add the negative representation of the number. Thus $5 - 3 = 2$ becomes $5 + (-3) = 2$. Does this work? Let's try it.

$$
\begin{aligned}
&\text{If } +5 = 0101 \\
&\qquad +3 = 0011 \\
&\text{and } -3 = 1011 \\
&\text{Then } +5 + (-3) \text{ becomes } 0101 \\
&\qquad\qquad\qquad\qquad\quad + 1011 \\
&\qquad\qquad\qquad\qquad\quad \overline{10000}
\end{aligned}
$$

It doesn't work. Either the method we have adopted for representing the sign does not work

or the method we have adopted for representing the numeric portion of the negative number does not work.

In order to find out what is wrong, let's look more carefully at negative numbers.

Sign Bit   The only way you can tell whether a binary digit is representing the sign of a number or a digit within the number is by looking at the binary digit position. **The leftmost bit position must be interpreted as the sign bit.**

How are you going to tell the difference between a signed binary number and an unsigned binary number that is one digit longer? The answer is that you cannot tell the difference by simple inspection. You simply have to know what you are dealing with. The necessity of interpreting numbers is, of course, not new to us. We discussed the interpretation of numbers in Chapter 2, when describing Susan Kilobyte's bill-paying program. Telling you that you must know in advance whether a binary number is signed or unsigned is much the same as telling you that you must differentiate between a dollar amount and the bank number on a check. This type of number interpretation is a constant necessity when dealing with microcomputers. You have to differentiate between signed and unsigned numeric data, as well as the many additional ways in which a sequence of bits (binary digits) might have to be interpreted. This causes the power and complexity of computer programming.

Returning to the signed binary numbers, as we have defined them, let us examine the sign bit critically. By selecting the off switch to represent either a plus sign or a 0 bit, positive signed binary numbers have the same numeric interpretation as unsigned binary numbers. This may be illustrated as follows:

Decimal Number		Binary Number
3_{10}	=	11_2
$+3_{10}$	=	011_2

Leading 0   When going from positive unsigned numbers to positive signed numbers we add a leading 0, which in no way affects the magnitude of the number. That means our representation of the sign is satisfactory. What about the numeric bits? We have one of the following two choices:

1. We can place a 1, representing the negative sign, to the left of the positive number high-order bit.

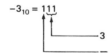

2. Alternatively, we can take the binary digit pattern created by subtracting the positive number from 0, as we did when we subtracted 3 from 0, and we can place the 1 to the left of the most significant numeric bit.

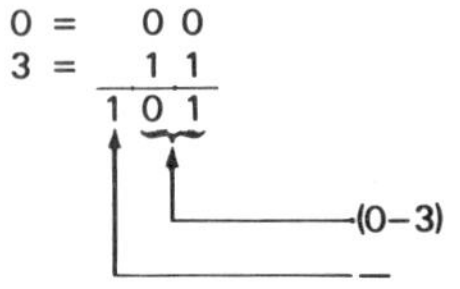

```
0 =    0 0
3 =    1 1
      1 0 1
```

(0-3)

It just so happens that method 1, which we automatically selected, does not work (as we demonstrated by trying to subtract 3 from 5). **Method 2 is the simplest way to go.** Using method 2, the following is how we would use four binary digits to represent numbers in the range +7 through −7:

Decimal Numbers		Binary Numbers	
Positive	Negative	Positive	Negative
0	0	0000	0000
1	1	0001	1111
2	2	0010	1110
3	3	0011	1101
4	4	0100	1100
5	5	0101	1011
6	6	0110	1010
7	7	0111	1001

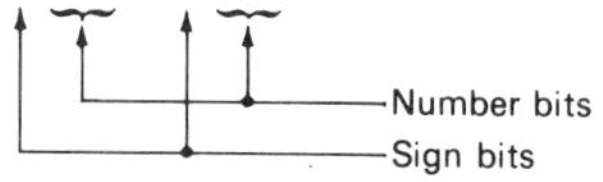

Number bits
Sign bits

Two's Complement

One's Complement

The representation of negative numbers illustrated above is referred to as the *two's complement* of the number.

In order to generate the two's complement of a number, you do not have to subtract the positive number from 0, then add a high-order (leftmost) 1 bit to represent the minus sign. There is a simpler procedure. **First, generate the one's complement of the number** by inverting every bit (binary digit); that is to say, replace 0 bits with 1 bits and 1 bits with 0 bits. The following are some examples of binary numbers and their one's complements:

Binary Number:	101	11101	101010
One's Complement:	010	00010	010101

Add 1 to the one's complement of the number and you have the two's complement of the number. Here are some examples, which you can verify against the negative binary numbers illustrated above.

```
            +3    =   0011
One's Complement  =   1100
Two's Complement  =   1101   =   -3

            +5    =   0101
One's Complement  =   1010
Two's Complement  =   1011   =   -5
```

Now let's see if this binary representation of negative numbers is valid. If it is, then **we must be able to subtract a number by adding its two's complement (that is, its negative representation).** Consider numbers in the range 1 through 7. If we make sure that we always subtract a smaller number from a larger number, then **the following are some examples which verify that we have developed a valid representation for negative numbers:**

Decimal	Binary
−7	1001
−6	1010
−5	1011
−4	1100
−3	1101
−2	1110
−1	1111
0	0000
1	0001
2	0010
3	0011
4	0100
5	0101
6	0110
7	0111

becomes

```
          7−3    =  4
becomes  7 + (−3)  =  4
          0 1 1 1
        + 1 1 0 1
        1 0 1 0 0
Carry
```

This is the binary form:

```
          5−1    =  4
becomes  5 + (−1)  =  4
          0 1 0 1
        + 1 1 1 1
        1 0 1 0 0
Carry
```

The result is valid, but there is a carry. Whenever a positive difference is generated by a subtraction, there is a carry of 1.

What happens **if you subtract a larger number from a smaller number?** Exactly the same thing that happens with decimal subraction. **You are left with a negative number.** For example, the following is what happens when you subtract 5 from 3:

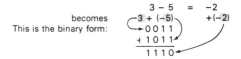

```
                     3 − 5   =  −2
       becomes     3 + (−5)    +(−2)
This is the binary form:
                     0 0 1 1
                   + 1 0 1 1
                     1 1 1 0
```

You can tell that the result is negative because the high-order digit of the binary result is 1. Remember that when you are dealing with positive and negative binary numbers, the high-order bit represents the sign of the number. If the high-order bit is 0, the number is positive; if the high-order bit is 1, as above, then the number is negative.

It is very easy to create the positive equivalent of a negative number. You simply take the two's complement of the negative number and you get back the positive number. Here are some examples of positive numbers, their two's complement negative equivalents, and regeneration of the original positive number.

```
                     +7   =   0111
    One's Complement      =   1000
    Two's Complement      =   1001   =   -7
    One's Complement      =   0110
    Two's Complement      =   0111   =   +7

                     +4   =   0100
    One's Complement      =   1011
    Two's Complement      =   1100   =   -4
    One's Complement      =   0011
    Two's Complement      =   0100   =   +4
```

There is nothing tricky about taking the two's complement of a number twice and getting the number back. After all, in the world of decimal arithmetic two negatives make a positive. For example, $-(-2)$ is $+2$. Thus, if the binary representation we have developed for negative numbers is valid, the two's complement of a negative number must give back the positive number, which it does.

We have developed a very elegant method of handling negative numbers and subtraction using binary digits, but remember, computers cannot cope with negative numbers. As long as you are using a computer, it is your responsibility to remember whether a binary digit pattern represents positive numbers only, or positive and negative numbers.

Binary Multiplication and Division

We are not going to discuss binary multiplication or division in much detail. This information will only be of value to you when you are a more experienced microcomputer user. There is, however, a very interesting phenomenon associated with multiplying and dividing binary numbers.

In order to multiply a binary number by 2, you shift each bit one place to the left. Here is an example.

$$27_{10} = 1B_{16} = 00011011_2$$
$$27_{10} \times 2 = 54_{10} = 36_{16} = 00110110_2$$

Shifting each bit of a binary number one position to the right is equivalent to dividing the number by 2. Here is an example.

$$36_{10} = 24_{16} = 00100100_2$$
$$18_{10} = 12_{16} = 00010010_2$$

There is nothing very surprising about shifting binary digits to multiply or divide by 2; you can do the same thing with decimal numbers. In order to multiply a decimal number by 10, you shift each digit one position to the left.

$$374 \times 10 = 3740$$

Shifting decimal digits one position to the right divides the number by 10.

$$\frac{26730}{10} = 2673$$

A number of methods have been devised to multiply and divide binary numbers. Some of these methods are described in the Osborne/ McGraw-Hill "Programming For Logic Design" series of books. If you program a microcomputer in a higher-level language, you never need to concern yourself with the exact procedure whereby binary numbers are multiplied; the compiler takes care of this chore for you. (Programming language options are discussed in the beginning of Chapter 5.) Why does anyone ever bother with assembly language? The answer, once again, is to have better control of your program.

There are, for example, many different programs you can write to perform binary multiplication or division. The various multiplication and division programs will all give you the same answer, but some of them execute very quickly while requiring a lot of memory to store the program, while others take a long time to execute but have relatively short programs. If you use a higher-level language, you take whatever multiplication or division program the language happens to give you. If you write your program, you can choose the multiplication or division method that is the fastest to execute, or the method that uses the least memory.

Octal and Hexadecimal Numbers

It takes a mathematical genius to convert multidigit decimal to binary numbers, but it is no problem for a microcomputer. A microcomputer works entirely with binary digits; it doesn't know decimal digits exist.

But for humans, **the manipulation of binary numbers is inconvenient, time-consuming and prone to error.** Imagine how easy it is to transpose a 0 and a 1 — and how hard it is to spot such an error. **This has resulted in the adoption of counting systems which are more compact than binary, yet have a simple relationship with binary digits. The two number systems most commonly used are** *octal* **and** *hexadecimal.*

Octal   **Every octal digit represents exactly three binary digits, as follows:**

Binary: 000 001 010 011 100 101 110 111
Octal: 0   1   2   3   4   5   6   7

The word *octal* **is derived from the number 8.** Octal numbers are *base 8* **numbers. Thus the numeral 10, which is 10 in the decimal counting system, is 8 in the octal counting system.**

You may look at the eight octal digits illustrated above and ask what difference there is between octal and decimal digits. There is none in the range 0 through 7, but octal digits have no 8 or 9. Thus, multioctal and multidecimal digits will not have the same values. This may be illustrated as follows:

Decimal	Octal
5	5
6	6
7	7
8	10
9	11
10	12
11	13
12	14

Octal numbers are identified by a trailing 8 subscript, as follows:

$$11_{10} = 13_8$$

11 (Decimal) = 13 (Octal)

Converting binary numbers into their octal equivalent is very straightforward. You simply partition the binary number into groups of three binary digits and replace each group of three binary digits with its octal digit equivalent. This may be illustrated as follows:

Binary: 110 101 110 111
Octal: 6   5   6   7

Thus

$$110101110111_2 = 6567_8$$

Conversely, if you want to convert an octal number to its binary equivalent, you simply replace each octal digit by its three-binary-digit equivalent. This may be illustrated as follows:

Octal: 2   5   7   4

Binary: 010 101 111 100

$2574_8 = 010101111100_2$

Hexadecimal

Every hexadecimal digit represents exactly four binary digits, as follows:

Binary:	0000	0001	0010	0011	0100	0101	0110	0111
Hexadecimal:	0	1	2	3	4	5	6	7
Decimal:	0	1	2	3	4	5	6	7

Binary:	1000	1001	1010	1011	1100	1101	1110	1111
Hexadecimal:	8	9	A	B	C	D	E	F
Decimal:	8	9	10	11	12	13	14	15

The word *hexadecimal* is derived from the number 16. Hexadecimal numbers are base 16 numbers. Thus, the numeral 10, which is 10 in a decimal counting system and 8 in an octal counting system, is 16 in a hexadecimal counting system. This poses a novel problem: if 10 represents 16 in the hexadecimal counting system, then **there must be 16 single numeric digits in the hexadecimal counting system,** just as there are ten single numeric digits in the decimal counting system. **The six additional hexadecimal single numeric digits are represented by the letters A, B, C, D, E, and F,** as illustrated above. Thus you must differentiate between the letters A through F representing either hexadecimal digits or letters of the alphabet. While this may seem to make things unnecessarily complicated, you will find it is never a problem. When you look at a piece of data, you know automatically whether you are looking at numbers or text; confusion will never arise.

You must understand that although octal and hexadecimal counting systems are useful to humans, computers are unaffected by the counting system you use, because **computers only recognize binary data.**

If microcomputers do not understand octal and hexadecimal number systems, can it really be easier for you to learn counting systems, rather than staying with decimal numbers and decimal-to-binary conversions? The answer is yes, you are better off learning octal and hexadecimal counting systems. Let's look at an example. The decimal number 2735 has the following binary, octal, and hexadecimal equivalents:

	A	A	F	Hexadecimal
Decimal 2735 =	1010	1010	1111	Binary
	5 2	5	7	Octal

We have described the standard techniques you can use to create binary digits out of decimal digits and vice versa. But these techniques are time-consuming and awkward to work with, no matter how well you understand binary and decimal numbers. On the other hand, you can convert between octal or hexadecimal numbers and their binary equivalents by inspection. Once you learn to think in octal and hexadecimal (and that is really quite easy), you will have the advantage of a short notation for writing data, and a simple conversion process for going to and from binary equivalents. This argument is much the same as the argument for metric measuring systems. There is no inherent difference between measuring distance in kilometers and meters, as against miles and yards; similarly, there is no inherent difference between decimal or hexadecimal counting. But in one case conversions are clumsy, while in the other they are straightforward.

Table 4-3 summarizes numbers in the range 0 through 16, showing their binary, decimal, octal, and hexadecimal representations.

The only aspect of octal and hexadecimal numbers with which you need to concern yourself is the conversion to binary or decimal numbers. Addition and subtraction using octal and hexadecimal numbers are identical to addition and subtraction using decimal numbers — bearing in mind, of course, that each numbering system has its own set of numeric digits.

Table 4-3. Number Systems

Hexadecimal	Decimal	Octal	Binary
0	0	0	0000
1	1	1	0001
2	2	2	0010
3	3	3	0011
4	4	4	0100
5	5	5	0101
6	6	6	0110
7	7	7	0111
8	8	10	1000
9	9	11	1001
A	10	12	1010
B	11	13	1011
C	12	14	1100
D	13	15	1101
E	14	16	1110
F	15	17	1111
10	16	20	10000

Octal-to-Hexadecimal Conversion

If you wish to convert from octal to hexadecimal or from hexadecimal to octal, the simplest way of doing it is via a binary intermediate step, since binary numbers have a digit-by-digit correlation with both octal and hexadecimal numbers. For example, consider the hexadecimal number $3C2F_{16}$. We may create its octal equivalent, using Table 4-3, as follows:

Hexadecimal:	3	C	2	F
Binary:	0011	1100	0010	1111
Octal:	0 3	6	0 5	7

Thus $3C2F_{16} = 36057_8$

You can convert the octal number 23754 to its hexadecimal equivalent as follows:

Octal:	2	3	7	5	4
Binary:	010	011	111	101	100
Hexadecimal:	2	7	E	C	

Thus $23754_8 = 27EC_{16}$

Decimal-to-Hexadecimal and Decimal-to-Octal Conversion

Converting a decimal number to its octal or hexadecimal equivalent follows the logic which we have already described for generating the binary equivalent of a decimal number.

Decimal to Hexadecimal **Consider first the conversion of a decimal number to its hexadecimal equivalent.** We make the conversion beginning with the least significant (that means the rightmost) digits. If our hexadecimal number is going to be a two-digit number, it would consist of 16 (the base) multiplied by some fixed digit (R) with a remainder of S.

$$RS_{16} = R_{10} \times 16_{10} + S_{10}$$

In order to find out what this remainder S is, we **divide the decimal number by the base (16) as follows:**

$$16 \,\overline{\big)\, NNN}$$
R remainder S

NNN is a decimal number; it is equal to the hexadecimal number RS_{16}. A real numeric example is as follows:

$$16 \underline{\smash{\big)}\, 124}$$
$$\text{7 remainder 12}$$

$$\text{Therefore } 124 = 7 \times 16 + 12$$
$$\text{so } 124_{10} = 7C_{16}$$

Thus, we are able to generate the digits R and S and we have a complete decimal-to-hexadecimal conversion. Decimal 124 equals hexadecimal 7C.

Now consider the larger decimal number 282_{10}. When we divide 282_{10} by 16_{10} this is what we get:

$$16 \underline{\smash{\big)}\, 282}$$
$$\text{17 remainder 10}$$

The remainder (S) is 10 decimal, which you will see from Table 4-3 has the hexadecimal equivalent A_{16}. So far so good. But R, the multiplier for the base, has the decimal equivalent 17. You will see from Table 4-3 that there is no single hexadecimal digit representing the decimal value 17. In order to generate the hexadecimal equivalent, therefore, we must go the next step and divide 17_{10} by 16_{10}.

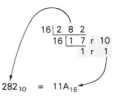

Decimal to Octal   **Let us convert the same two decimal numbers, 124_{10} and 282_{10}, to their octal equivalents.** Since octal numbers are base 8, we must repeatedly divide the decimal number by 8_{10} in order to generate the octal equivalent. This may be illustrated as follows:

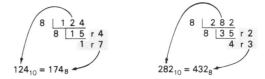

Now we can make sure that our conversions are correct by checking the octal and hexadecimal equivalents of 124_{10} and 282_{10} via their binary intermediate.

$$\begin{array}{ccc} 1 & 7 & 4 \\ \multicolumn{3}{c}{001111100} \\ \hline 0 & 7 & C \end{array} \qquad \begin{array}{ccc} 4 & 3 & 2 \\ \multicolumn{3}{c}{100011010} \\ \hline 1 & 1 & A \end{array}$$

$$124_{10} = 174_8 = 7C_{16} \qquad 282_{10} = 432_8 = 11A_{16}$$

Octal or Hexadecimal to Decimal

The octal and hexadecimal conversions are indeed correct.

Converting octal and hexadecimal numbers to their decimal equivalents is easy enough if you remember what the various digits of an octal or hexadecimal number represent. In order to keep things simple, consider four-digit numbers. The decimal representation of any four-digit number may be defined by the following equation:

Decimal value = $P \times (Base)^3 + Q \times (Base)^2 + R \times Base + S$

A number with more than four digits would simply have terms to the left with higher powers of the base. Now the general four-digit equation can be rewritten for the specific cases of octal and hexadecimal numbers as follows:

Decimal value = $P \times 8^3 + Q \times 8^2 + R \times 8 + S$ for octal numbers

Decimal value = $P \times 16^3 + Q \times 16^2 + R \times 16 + S$ for hexadecimal numbers

In order to convert an octal or hexadecimal number to its decimal equivalent, you multiply each digit of the octal or hexadecimal number by the appropriate base multiplier. Here are some examples:

$$\begin{aligned} 2473_8 &= (2 \times (8)^3 + 4 \times 8^2 + 7 \times 8 + 3)_{10} \\ &= (2 \times 512 + 4 \times 64 + 7 \times 8 + 3)_{10} \\ &= (1024 + 256 + 56 + 3)_{10} \\ &= 1339_{10} \end{aligned}$$

$$\begin{aligned} 149A_{16} &= (1 \times 16^3 + 4 \times 16^2 + 9 \times 16 + 10)_{10} \\ &= (1 \times 4096 + 4 \times 256 + 9 \times 16 + 10)_{10} \\ &= (4096 + 1024 + 144 + 10) \\ &= 5274_{10} \end{aligned}$$

Character Codes

The two-state switches that microcomputer logic uses to generate binary digits must also be used to represent letters of the alphabet and any character capable of being displayed, printed or otherwise handled. If, as we stated at the beginning of this chapter, computer logic consists of nothing more than an array of two-state switches, then **in order to represent characters, we must use switch (and, therefore, binary digit) patterns.**

In order to come up with some reasonable character coding technique we must explore the following two problems:

1. Is there any "natural" method of representing characters, as there is for representing binary data?

2. How will we distinguish between a binary digit pattern representing a character as opposed to the binary digit pattern representing numbers or any other information?

There is no "natural" method of representing characters using binary digit codes, and any binary digit code that we generate could also be interpreted as a binary number. Once again you, as a programmer, need to know in advance what a binary numeric digit sequence represents. And once again you can rest assured that this multiple use of binary never creates problems.

The various codes used to represent characters all use a byte (eight binary digits) to represent a single character. A byte has 256 different possible combinations of eight binary digits.

```
      7  6  5  4  3  2  1  0  ◄──── Bit Number
     ┌──┬──┬──┬──┬──┬──┬──┬──┐
     │  │  │  │  │  │  │  │  │ ◄──── A byte
     └──┴──┴──┴──┴──┴──┴──┴──┘
      0  0  0  0  0  0  0  0        0  ┐
      0  0  0  0  0  0  0  1        1  │
      0  0  0  0  0  0  1  0        2  │
      ─  ─  ─  ─  ─  ─  ─  ─        ─  │
      1  0  0  0  0  0  0  1      129  ├ Decimal value
      1  0  0  0  0  0  1  0      130  │ of bit pattern
      1  0  0  0  0  0  1  1      131  │
      ─  ─  ─  ─  ─  ─  ─  ─        ─  │
      1  1  1  1  1  1  0  1      253  │
      1  1  1  1  1  1  1  0      254  │
      1  1  1  1  1  1  1  1      255  ┘
```

Thus a byte may be interpreted as

· A positive number with a decimal value in the range
  0 through +255

· A signed number with a decimal value in the range
  −128 through +127

· One byte of a multibyte signed or unsigned number

· A character code

ASCII   **The most popular coding scheme used to represent characters is known as the American Standard Code for Information Interchange,**

generally referred to by the letters *ASCII.* The complete ASCII code set for all printable characters is given in Appendix A.

Only the ASCII character codes for the numeric digits 0 through 9 have a logical basis for their selection. If you look at these character codes, you will see that the four low-order binary digits equal the numeric value associated with the character.

Binary Code	Hexadecimal Equivalent	ASCII Character
00110000	30	0
00110001	31	1
00110010	32	2
00110011	33	3
00110100	34	4
00110101	35	5
00110110	36	6
00110111	37	7
00111000	38	8
00111001	39	9

Notice that in Appendix A we show the binary digit pattern representing every character code using its hexadecimal equivalent. This makes the character codes far easier to read. **We can show the numeric equivalent of a text string using hexadecimal digits as follows:**

```
T    h    i    s         i    s         t    h    e         n    u    m    e    r    i    c
54   68   69   73   20   69   73   20   74   68   65   20   6E   75   6D   65   72   69   63   0D

e    q    u    i    v    a    l    e    n    t         o    f         a
65   71   75   69   76   61   6C   65   6E   74   20   6F   66   20   61   0D

t    e    x    t         s    t    r    i    n    g    .
24   65   78   74   20   73   74   72   69   6E   67   2E
```

Each of the text letters has beneath it the two hexadecimal digits which represent the ASCII code for the letter, as defined in Appendix A. Notice that the hexadecimal code 20_{16} appears between words. This is the code for a space. The code $0D_{16}$ represents a carriage return.

String **The word *string* is commonly used to describe a sequence of characters stored via their numeric codes. That is why we referred to the text above as a *text string.***

Within a computer your text will be stored as a sequence of bits (binary digits). When you want to print this text, fetch the bits in the proper sequence and transmit them to a display or printer. Logic associated with the display or printer interprets the binary data, assuming that it represents characters.

If you enter text via a keyboard, then each time you depress a key, **the binary digit code associated with that key is transmitted to the microcomputer,** which stores the code in appropriate memory.

You can modify character codes by treating them as binary data. Suppose, for example, that you have a large amount of numeric data which you wish to store in memory, and you have no alphabetic data. If you look again at the ASCII table in Appendix A, you will see that all decimal digits have the same four high-order bits.

ASCII code for decimal digit N is $3N_{16}$.

Packed Bytes   **You could save a lot of memory by packing decimal digits, two per byte, as follows:**

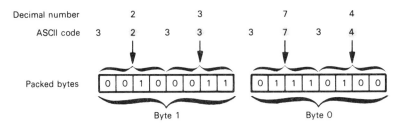

By performing the operations illustrated in Figure 4-1 on your character codes, you can recreate the ASCII characters.

Computer Logic and Boolean Operations

A microcomputer will spend very little of its time doing arithmetic. In fact, there are many programs that contain no arithmetic whatsoever. A computer will spend most of its time performing "logical" operations.

Status Flags

If you examine flowcharts for program logic, you will frequently see the following type of decision step:

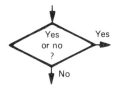

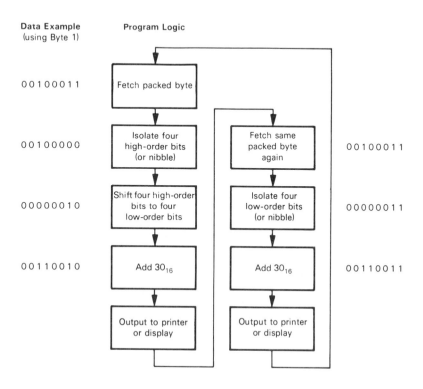

One common method for handling simple two-way decision logic, as illustrated above, is to provide the microcomputer with some special switches called *status flags*. Events preceding the logic step must place one of these switches off or on. The two-way decision-making logic then becomes a single instruction, which may be illustrated as follows:

"If flag is on, branch to instruction x.
If flag is off, continue with the next instruction."

Status flags represent one of the simplest forms of microcomputer logic. Different microcomputers have different numbers and types of status flags, but identifying them individually is unnecessary at this point. In order to understand the concept of a status flag, all you need to think of is a two-way switch which instructions in your program can turn on or off; subsequent instructions in your program test the

switch in order to determine which of two paths your program logic
will take. This may be illustrated as follows:

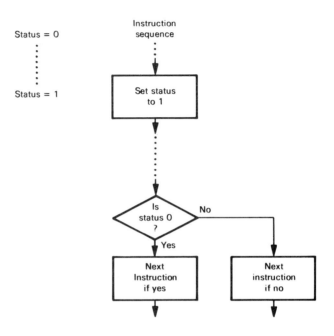

Logical Operators

Logical
Operators

Most computer logic is generated by four *logical operators*. There is
nothing very mysterious about logical operators; addition, subtraction, multiplication, and division are *arithmetic operators*. A logical
operator takes data input, does something nonarithmetic to it, and
creates a result — just as an arithmetic operator takes data input,
does something arithmetic to it, and generates a result.

There are four logical operators: the NOT, AND, OR, and
Exclusive-OR operators. We will discuss each logical operator in
turn.

The NOT Operator

The NOT operator is the simplest to understand. This operator simply
says: move a switch to its opposite setting; that is, if it is on, turn it off
and if it is off, turn it on. Looking at the effect of a NOT operator on a

bit (binary digit), it **converts a 1 to a 0 or a 0 to a 1.** This may be illustrated as follows:

$$
\begin{aligned}
\text{NOT } 0 &= 1 \\
\text{NOT } 1 &= 0 \\
\text{NOT } 101101 &= 010010
\end{aligned}
$$

**Frequently, a bar over a number is used instead of the NOT. This
may be illustrated as follows:**

$$
\begin{aligned}
\overline{0} &= 1 \\
\overline{1} &= 0 \\
\overline{101101} &= 010010
\end{aligned}
$$

**One's
Complement**
The NOT operator creates the one's complement of a number.
Remember, the first step in creating the two's complement of a number
is to create the one's complement of the number.

The AND Operator

**The AND operator tests for two switches both being on. AND opera-
tions may be defined as follows:**

$$
\begin{aligned}
0 \text{ AND } 0 &= 0 \\
0 \text{ AND } 1 &= 0 \\
1 \text{ AND } 0 &= 0 \\
1 \text{ AND } 1 &= 1
\end{aligned}
$$

A dot ($\cdot$) is frequently used instead of the word AND. The four AND
operations illustrated above may therefore be rewritten as follows:

$$
\begin{aligned}
0 \cdot 0 &= 0 \\
0 \cdot 1 &= 0 \\
1 \cdot 0 &= 0 \\
1 \cdot 1 &= 1
\end{aligned}
$$

AND operation logic is a common part of our everyday lives. For
example, I have two small sons, Ian and Paul, both of whom like to
argue. When shopping at the supermarket, if the two boys can buy just
one candy bar, then the candy bar will be selected on the basis of the
AND operation. That is to say, we buy candy bar X only if Ian wants
candy bar X AND Paul wants candy bar X.

Ian wants candy bar A and
Paul wants candy bar X. $A \cdot X = 0$
No candy bar selected.

Ian wants candy bar X and
Paul wants candy bar X. $X \cdot X = 1$
Buy candy bar X.

If either Ian or Paul rejects a candy bar, then the candy bar will not be
selected.

Bit Mask   We have also seen a microcomputer application for the AND operation. Recall that we explained how numeric digit character codes can be stored two per byte. In Figure 4-1, **you could use an 8-bit mask and an AND operation in order to isolate one or the other numeric nibble.** This may be illustrated for byte 1 of Figure 4-1 as follows:

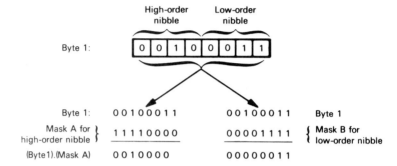

Wherever a 0 bit must be inserted in a sequence of data bits, we provide a 0 bit in an AND mask. Wherever the AND mask has a 1 bit, it passes data bits through unaltered. For example, suppose you want to preserve bits 2, 3, 4, and 5 of a byte, but you want bits 0, 1, 6, and 7 to be 0. You would AND your binary data with the mask 00111100. This may be illustrated as follows:

```
  Binary data:  7  6  5  4  3  2  1  0  ◄──────Bit No.
        Mask:   X  X  X  X  X  X  X  X
Data AND Mask:  0  0  1  1  1  1  0  0
                ─────────────────────
                0  0  X  X  X  X  0  0
```

The OR Operator

The OR logical operation is a test for *any* on switch. The OR operation may be defined as follows:

```
0 OR 0  =  0
0 OR 1  =  1
1 OR 0  =  1
1 OR 1  =  1
```

The plus sign (+) is frequently used instead of OR. The four OR operations illustrated above may therefore be rewritten as follows:

```
0 + 0  =  0
0 + 1  =  1
1 + 0  =  1
1 + 1  =  1
```

The fact that a plus sign may be used to represent the OR logical operator may confuse you, but it is irrelevant to a computer. There will be distinct instructions with their own independent instruction codes, representing an addition operation or a logical OR operation. The plus sign used to represent addition or a logical OR operation will occur only in printed or written material.

The OR operation is also a familiar part of our daily lives. For example, when stocking up on breakfast cereals at the supermarket, I will buy cereal X if either Ian OR Paul wants it.

Does Ian want cereal X?		Does Paul want cereal X?		Buy cereal X?
No (=0)	+	No (=0)	=	No (=0)
No (=0)	+	Yes (=1)	=	Yes (=1)
Yes (=1)	+	No (=0)	=	Yes (=1)
Yes (=1)	+	Yes (=1)	=	Yes (=1)

We can use the OR operator on our decimal digit character example (Figure 4-1) in order **to provide the four high-order bits of the character's ASCII code.** This may be illustrated as follows:

```
                                    7  6  5  4  3  2  1  0 ◄────Bit Number
                 Isolated nibble:   0  0  0  0  0  0  1  1
OR mask for high-order four bits:   0  0  1  1  0  0  0  0
                                    0  0  1  1  0  0  1  1
```

Wherever a 1 bit must be inserted in a sequence of data bits, we provide a 1 bit in an OR mask. Wherever the OR mask has a 0 bit, it passes data bits through unaltered. This may be illustrated as follows:

```
                  7  6  5  4  3  2  1  0 ◄──Bit No.
   Binary data:   X  X  X  X  X  X  X  X
Arbitrary mask:   0  0  1  1  1  1  0  0
  Data OR mask:   X  X  1  1  1  1  X  X
```

Thus, the AND operator may be used as a *clearing mask* **while the OR operator may be used as an** *inserting mask.*

The XOR Operator

The last logical operator we will describe is the Exclusive-OR, or XOR. The Exclusive-OR tests for differences and changes; it may be defined as follows:

```
0 XOR 0 = 0
0 XOR 1 = 1
1 XOR 0 = 1
1 XOR 1 = 0
```

The ⊕ symbol is frequently used instead of the letters XOR. Thus, the four XOR operations illustrated above may be rewritten as follows:

$$0 \oplus 0 = 0$$
$$0 \oplus 1 = 1$$
$$1 \oplus 0 = 1$$
$$1 \oplus 1 = 0$$

The Exclusive-OR is also a part of our daily logical lives; it identifies differences of opinion. For example, a fight results when Ian says yes and Paul says no.

Ian's opinion		Paul's opinion		Fight?
No (=0)	⊕	No (=0)	=	No (=0)
No (=0)	⊕	Yes (=1)	=	Yes (=1)
Yes (=1)	⊕	No (=0)	=	Yes (=1)
Yes (=1)	⊕	Yes (=1)	=	No (=0)

In computer logic you will use the Exclusive-OR operation to check for changes in state. Suppose, for example, knowing that a switch is on or off is insufficient; you also need to know whether the switch has been switched on or off since you last tested it. You can save the condition of any switch each time you test it, then compare the switch position with the saved condition as follows:

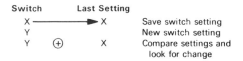

Switch		Last Setting	
X	⟶	X	Save switch setting
Y			New switch setting
Y	⊕	X	Compare settings and look for change

Thus, by performing an Exclusive-OR operation on the switch condition and its previous setting, you can find out whether the switch changed since you last tested it.

5
Inside a Microcomputer

In Chapters 1, 2, and 3 we described overall microcomputer concepts, and in Chapter 4 we defined the basic concepts out of which any computer function can be created. It is now time to bridge the gap between the fundamental concepts and the end product — the microcomputer system. We are going to bridge this gap in the next two chapters. In this chapter we will look at the microcomputer itself, separating and exploring its various components; in Chapter 6, we will describe how the basic digital logic concepts of Chapter 4 can be used to create the components of the microcomputer system described in this chapter.

In order to examine the functional components of a microcomputer we begin by looking at the way in which a microcomputer may be programmed using a programming language.

Programming Languages

Programming is done with so-called *higher-level* languages such as BASIC, FORTRAN, and COBOL. There are also fundamental programming languages referred to as *assembly language.*

When regarding any programming language, the most important point to understand is that **a programming language is a programmer's convenience,** an artificial creation designed to make your life as a programmer easier. However, with whatever language you use, **the computer still demands that it receive the program as a sequence of numbers.**

The computer itself will convert the program from the form in which you, the programmer, write it to the form in which it can understand and execute the program. In order to make this conversion, the computer executes another program — a program that someone else wrote for you.

Assembler   A program called **an *assembler* converts programs that you write in assembly language** into programs which the computer can understand and execute.

Compiler   A program referred to as **a *compiler* performs the same conversion task for programs that you write using a higher-level language.**

Assemblers and compilers treat your program as data; they read it in as data and convert it to another form of data that enables the computer to execute your program.

Source Program   **We refer to a program that we can actually read as a *source program,*** that is, a source program is written in a programming language. **Once the program has been converted to enable the computer to read it, it is called an *object program.*** An object program is nothing but a

Object Program   sequence of numbers.

Thus, assemblers and compilers read in data (your source program) and convert it to another form of data (an object program).

There are two types of compilers. One type converts your program into a form the computer can read and saves this form. Subsequently, the computer-readable form is loaded into memory for execution. This may be illustrated as follows:

Step 1 — The Compiling Step

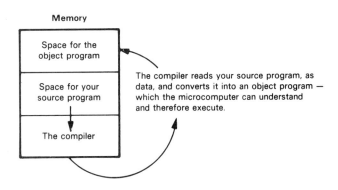

Memory

Space for the object program

Space for your source program

The compiler

The compiler reads your source program, as data, and converts it into an object program — which the microcomputer can understand and therefore execute.

Step 2 — The Execution Step

Memory

```
┌─────────────────────┐
│                     │
│     The object      │
│      program        │
│                     │
├─────────────────────┤
│                     │
│   Memory space      │
│    you can use      │
│    for data, or     │
│  any other purpose  │
│                     │
│                     │
└─────────────────────┘
```

Interpreter   **The other type of compiler never saves the computer-readable form of your program (the object program). This type of compiler is called an *interpreter*.** When you use an interpreter, your whole source program resides in memory, along with the interpreter, for as long as the source program is being executed. This may be illustrated as follows:

Memory

```
┌─────────────────────┐
│   Memory space      │
│     for data        │
├─────────────────────┤
│   Your source       │
│   program is        │
│   stored here       │
├─────────────────────┤
│   The interpreter   │
│   is stored here    │
└─────────────────────┘
```

The interpreter converts your source program into object code as it is needed.

The following illustration shows an area of memory being set aside for your whole source program. You might be misled into thinking that the amount of memory set aside for your source program puts an upper limit on the size of the source program you can execute. In fact, you can execute much larger programs as long as the larger program can be broken into blocks, where no one block overflows the available source program memory space.

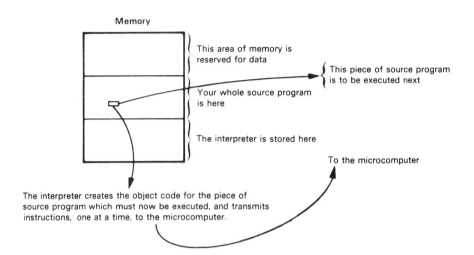

Memory

This area of memory is reserved for data

This piece of source program is to be executed next

Your whole source program is here

The interpreter is stored here

To the microcomputer

The interpreter creates the object code for the piece of source program which must now be executed, and transmits instructions, one at a time, to the microcomputer.

Compilers and interpreters are themselves object programs that someone else wrote for you.

We can explain the difference between a compiler and an interpreter without technical terms by thinking of the ways in which an actor may learn to deliver lines in a play. Think of the source program as the actor's script; object program instructions going to the microcomputer are equivalent to the actor's delivery of lines to an audience. If the actor learns the entire part, then throws away the script and delivers the lines, what he has done is equivalent to compiling a source program. But suppose the actor does not learn the entire part. Suppose the actor keeps the script and has a prompter display the lines one at a time using prompting boards. He is now delivering his lines in the fashion of an interpreter.

BASIC is the most popular microcomputer higher-level language, as well as being an interpreter language.

Higher-Level Language

In summary, we can divide most programming languages into higher-level languages and assembly language. Higher-level languages are converted into object programs by compilers and interpreters. Assembly languages are converted into object code by an assembler.

Assembly Languages

Higher-level languages are designed to represent problems, while assembly languages are designed to represent the computer. Thus, a computer views a higher-level language source program as an alien thing, and the compiler must convert the source program into an object program. In contrast, an assembly language source program can be converted into an object program easily; an assembler is therefore a relatively simple program. We will now compare higher-level languages and assembly language in order to more clearly identify differences between the two.

A Comparison of Higher-Level Languages And Assembly Language

Advantages of Higher-Level Languages
We will first look at the advantages of higher-level languages.

Higher-level languages are easier to use than assembly language because higher-level languages represent the problem rather than the computer. For example, a simple addition would be written in the following self-evident form using a higher-level language:

SUM = VAL1+VAL2

VAL1 and VAL2 are names you assign to an augend and an addend — they can have any values. SUM is the name you assign to the sum.

Assembly language presents you with a definition of your computer in a form you can read. Thus, the addition illustrated above would be programmed in assembly language as follows:

```
LXI     H,VAL1
LDA     VAL2
ADD     A,M
STA     SUM
```

VAL1 and VAL2 are no longer names you assign to the augend and addend. VAL1 and VAL2 are now addresses: they identify memory locations in which the augend and addend are stored. Thus, the augend and addend must each be small enough to fit within one memory location. SUM, likewise, is the address of the memory location where the sum will be stored, provided it will fit into one memory word.

The assembly language definition of the addition is by no means self-evident.

Another important advantage of higher-level languages is that the language is not designed with any computer in mind. **If you write a program in a higher-level language, you can convert this higher-level language source program to an object program that will run on any computer, provided the computer has a compiler (or interpreter) for your higher-level language.** Suppose you write a program in BASIC. You can execute this BASIC program on your computer, and all of your friends can execute your program on totally different computers if their computers also have BASIC interpreters. This may be illustrated as follows.

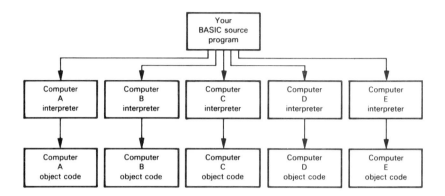

Assembly Language Programming

Assembly language, on the other hand, is a human representation of the computer you are using. Thus, every single computer and microprocessor has its own, unique assembly language; and a program written in an assembly language for one computer or microprocessor is totally unintelligible to any other computer or microprocessor. If you write an assembly language source program for your microprocessor, only people with microcomputers containing your microprocessor will be able to assemble and run your source program.

In theory it is possible to write a program (much like a compiler) that would take a source program written in one microprocessor's assembly language and convert it into an object program for another microprocessor. In reality few people do this, since another microprocessor's assembly language is as strange and hard to deal with as a higher-level language.

Advantages of Assembly Language

With all the advantages that result from programming in a higher-level language, why would anyone bother with assembly language? Assembly language also has advantages.

Assembly language generates shorter object programs than do higher-level languages because the assembly language for each microprocessor or computer is designed specifically for that microprocessor or computer. In fact, an object program created by a compiler from a higher-level language source program is usually two to four times longer than the same object program created by an assembler from an assembly language source program. The reason for this is that the compiler must write an assembly language program to represent the problem as defined in the higher-level language. But while a human programmer can write an assembly language using human judgment, a compiler must do the job by fixed rules.

Consider an everyday analogy. You are asked to give someone directions to drive from one point to another in a city. If you know the exact source and destination, and the exact city, you can define a very direct route.

"Basic map reproduced by permission of the California State Automobile Association, copyright owner."

Now try to create a set of general-purpose instructions which you can string together in order to define the route to be driven between any two points in any city. These instructions, if they are to be interpreted by a machine, can leave nothing to the imagination. Thus, there must be some fixed number of instructions such as

```
Turn left
Turn right
Test for a one-way street
Test for a one way street
Test for a dead end road
Test for a 45° turn
etc.
```

You cannot include instructions that assume you know whether a street is one way, since one-way streets are subject to change. You cannot include instructions that simply define the number of blocks to travel in a straight line, since there may be barriers in the road preventing such travel. (Or in cities with steep hills, such as San Francisco, a road which appears to be continuous in reality has a 100-foot (30-meter) precipice dividing it at some point.)

Once you start devising a set of general-purpose direction rules that take into account undefinable contingencies, you will have some idea of the problems faced by a compiler. The compiler does not know what the peculiarities of any specific computer may be; therefore, it must generate programs that take into account the strangest possibilities.

Disadvantages of Higher-Level Languages

Higher-level languages have another problem. The compiler that converts a higher-level language source program to an object program is itself a large program. A compiler program may be eight times longer than an assembler program. Thus, **until your microcomputer system is quite large, you cannot use a higher-level language since your microcomputer system will have insufficient memory to hold the compiler.**

If you have an interpreter, then the interpreter must always be in memory together with the problem you are executing. This difference between a compiler and an interpreter was illustrated earlier in this chapter.

Because higher-level language source programs generate longer object programs and there are more instructions to be executed, the object programs will take longer to execute. If your application is running too long, you can speed things up by a factor of two or more by simply rewriting your program in assembly language.

But some of the advantages associated with higher-level languages are not all they appear to be. For example, **higher-level languages are supposed to be portable** (that is, one higher-level language source program can be compiled and executed by many different microprocessors). This is not always true. **Frequently you will find that there** are minor differences in the way one computer's compiler expects the source program to appear. However, even in the worst case, the changes you would make to convert to a higher-level language source program when going to a new microprocessor or computer are tiny compared to the problems associated with completely rewriting the program in the new microprocessor's or computer's assembly language.

What is our conclusion?

If you are going to use a microcomputer simply as a vehicle for executing programs, you should go to higher-level languages as quickly as you can. If, on the other hand, you plan to thoroughly understand the microcomputer itself — building your own, changing it, extending it, or otherwise playing with its components — then you should learn assembly language as quickly as possible. Once you know assembly language you will probably stay with assembly language.

Microcomputer Functional Logic

The object program you create determines the functions that will be performed by the logic of your microcomputer.

Figure 5-1 illustrates the logic of a microcomputer; this is the logic which we are now going to discuss.

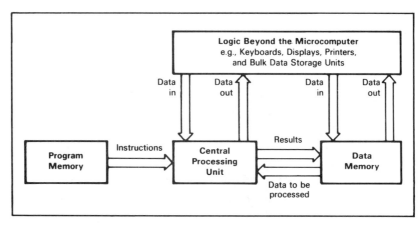

Figure 5-1. Microcomputer Functional Logic

It does not matter what the microcomputer is ultimately going to do — the task consists of the following three steps:

1. **Bringing data into the microcomputer**
2. **Modifying the data**
3. **Transmitting the modified data back out from the microcomputer.**

Logic beyond the microcomputer (which consists of physical units we described earlier in this book) is used to enter information, receive results, and store large quantities of data. Data that is in the process of being operated on is stored in data memory, which you will recall from Chapter 3 is fast access, read/write memory. Therefore, **steps 1 and 3 above are handled by the shaded microcomputer logic shown in Figure 5-2.**

Physical units transmit information to and from the microcomputer via appropriate interface logic. With reference to Figure 5-1 this may be illustrated as follows:

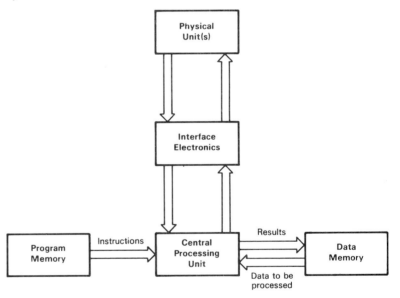

Central Processing Unit Operations that are actually performed on data are performed by logic within the Central Processing Unit (CPU). These operations are defined by a sequence of instructions that taken together constitute a program. The program is stored in program memory. Thus, **step 2 of the above three steps is handled by the shaded microcomputer logic shown in Figure 5-3.**

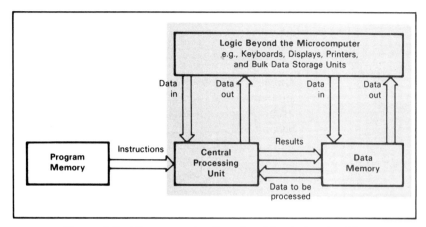

Figure 5-2. Microcomputer Functional Logic Involved In
Data Movement and Storage

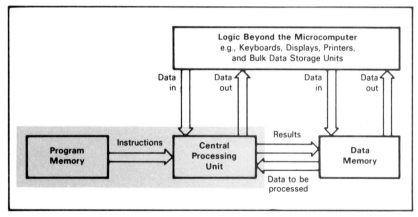

Figure 5-3. Microcomputer Functional Logic Involved In
Data Modification

**Program
Memory**
    **Program memory can be read-only memory, or it can be read/write
memory.** Program memory can be read-only memory because instructions are transmitted from the program stored in program memory to
the central processing unit, but instructions are usually not transmitted
from the CPU to program memory. Program memory does not have to
be read-only memory. It is common practice in microcomputer systems
to separate programs from data, as shown in Figure 5-1, and in many

industrial microcomputer applications, programs are held in read-only memory to ensure that the program is never accidentally changed or lost.

But **program memory and data memory could be one and the same memory.** Moreover, it is possible for one part of a program to treat another part of the program as data, in which case the program changes itself. As you might expect, programs that change themselves can become very complex, so, at least while you are a beginner, it is wise to think of program memory and data memory as distinct entities.

The fact that you do not yet have a good understanding of how program and data memories work is unimportant. Program and data memory can store information in a form that can be read by the computer. For now, that is all you need to know about program and data memory.

Information Paths

Let us now consider the various information paths shown in Figure 5-1.

When the CPU is modifying data, it fetches the data to be modified from data memory, and it returns the results to data memory. **Therefore, there are paths in both directions between data memory and the CPU.**

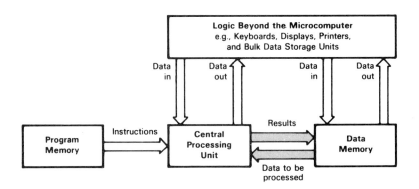

New data entering the microcomputer travels from external physical units to data memory via the CPU. **Results being output** travel from memory via the CPU to external physical units. This may be illustrated as follows:

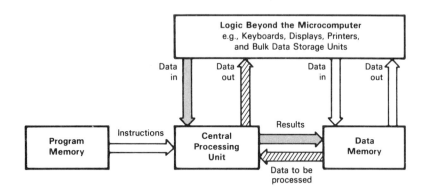

High-speed information transfer between a floppy disk and data memory frequently occurs directly between these two devices, bypassing the CPU.

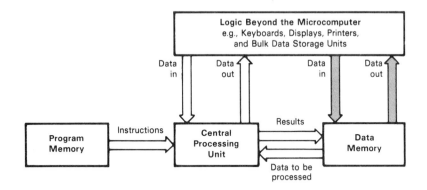

Direct Memory Access   The data path illustrated above is referred to as Direct Memory Access. Direct Memory Access is usually referred to by its initials, *DMA*. While memory has to be at one end of the DMA data transfer, a floppy disk need not be at the other end, even though it frequently is. Any external logic may provide the other end of the DMA data transfer.

Whenever the CPU is doing something — moving data or modifying data — a stream of instructions transmitted from program memory to the CPU controls CPU operations. Thus, **there must be a unidirectional path for information to flow from program memory to the CPU.**

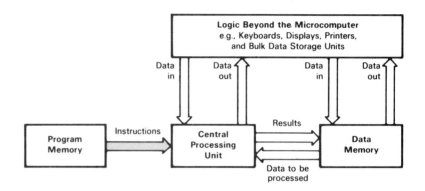

The Central Processing Unit

Central to all microcomputer logic is the Central Processing Unit. The CPU is the electronic logic that actually performs all operations on data; that is to say, in various other parts of the microcomputer system, you can move data from one location to another, but only within the CPU can you actually change data.

Serial Logic

In order to generate the versatility and power commonly associated with computers, CPU logic must be capable of performing a large number of different operations. That is what the CPU can do. However, the CPU can only perform one operation at a time.

Augend   Consider the addition of two numbers: when two numbers are added, they are called the augend and the addend. The augend and the

Addend   addend are summed via the following serial sequence of events.

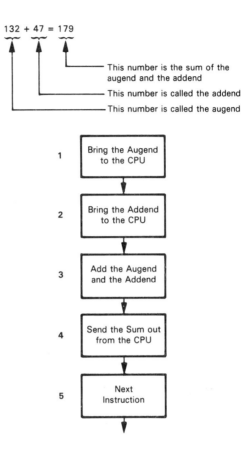

Each event is identified by a number, 1, 2, 3, 4, and so forth. The CPU performs each event as a single operation. Therefore, in order to perform the addition illustrated above, the **CPU performs event 1, then event 2, then event 3, then event 4.**

· During step 1 the augend is brought to the CPU

· During step 2 the addend is brought to the CPU

· During step 3 the augend and addend are summed by electronic logic within the CPU

· During step 4 the sum is transmitted out from the CPU.

These four steps are essentially identical to the four steps by which you add two numbers using some types of pocket calculators.

During step 1 you will key in the augend.

During step 2 you will key in the addend.

During step 3 you will press the + key.

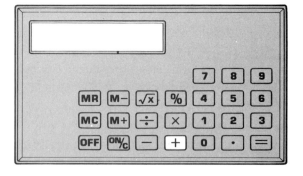

Step 4 occurs automatically: the sum is output from the logic of the calculator to a display where you can read it.

Now you know why some calculations make you do things awkwardly; they force you to use computer logic sequences.

Many calculators use a more complex logic that lets you work in algebraic sequence, which is the way we learned arithmetic.

· During step 1 you key in the augend or first number

· During step 2 you press the + key

· During step 3 you key in the addend or second number

· Step 4 occurs automatically: the sum is output.

Serial Devices

We can use the four calculator steps (either version) for adding two numbers to illustrate the concept of a serial device since a calculator and a CPU are both *serial devices* — each can perform just one operation at a time. This is simple enough to understand in the case of a simple calculator; you cannot, for example, simultaneously key in the two numbers which are to be added. The two numbers must be keyed in serially, one after the other. In the case of a CPU, you cannot simultaneously bring the augend and the addend to the CPU; each number must be fetched in an independent step, and the two steps must occur one after the other.

Serial Logic Step

Instruction Step

The next problem that we are going to encounter is determining what a single *step* consists of. In the case of the calculator, this is not a very important consideration. For example, when you enter the number 132 via the keys, does entry of the entire number constitute one *step?* Or does each keystroke constitute an individual *step?* Frankly, this question is inconsequential. But what if you have to write down a sequence of instructions that someone else must follow? You could write down the following single step:

· Enter 132 at the keyboard

You could break up the one step into the following three separate steps:

· Press the 1 key
· Press the 3 key
· Press the 2 key

Consider an even more mundane example: eating a piece of cake.

Suppose a piece of cake can be eaten in ten mouthfuls. Is eating this piece of cake a ten-step process? Eating a single mouthful of cake may itself consist of the following four steps:

· Separate a piece of cake with your fork
· Impale the separated piece of cake on the end of your fork
· Transfer the separated piece of cake to your mouth
· Chew and swallow the piece of cake.

Instructions   It would be easy to subdivide these four cake-eating steps, creating any number of additional smaller steps. The same is true of single CPU steps. Some CPUs perform operations in relatively big steps; others sequence events as a series of relatively small steps. But **for every CPU, every step is clearly and unambiguously defined as an *instruction.*** There is nothing vague about an individual instruction, or step, that can be executed by any CPU.

Instruction   **Every CPU responds to a fixed number of instructions. These**
Set   **instructions, taken together, are referred to as an *instruction set.*** Typically, a CPU will have from 40 to 200 different instructions in its instruction set.

Every instruction is represented by a unique number that, when transmitted to the CPU at the proper time, causes the CPU to execute the operations associated with the instruction. For example, our addition sequence may be illustrated as follows.

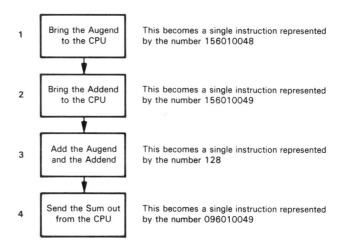

CPU Logical Data Storage

The four instructions shown above illustrate a logistic problem associated with the CPU.

The CPU has storage space to hold the data that it is about to operate on, and that is all. This may be illustrated as follows:

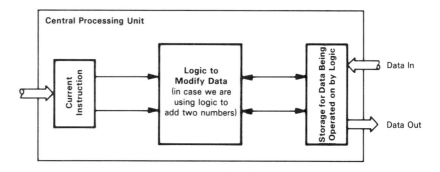

You cannot expect to leave the augend, addend, and sum in the CPU data storage space because you will almost certainly need this space for the very next operation the CPU performs. The augend, the addend, and the sum must, therefore, have permanent storage locations somewhere beyond the CPU — for example, in external read/write memory.

Program Memory

Program In order to perform any operation, such as the illustrated addition, you must create a sequence of instructions that taken together constitute a program. The program is a sequence of numbers. This sequence of numbers is stored in a fast-access memory that we call program memory. Using arbitrarily assigned number codes for the addition instruction, **the addition program may be represented conceptually as follows:**

```
Program
Memory

 ┌─────┐
 │ 156 │ ⎫
 ├─────┤ ⎬ 1
 │ 010 │ ⎮
 ├─────┤ ⎭
 │ 048 │
 ├─────┤ ⎫
 │ 156 │ ⎮
 ├─────┤ ⎬ 2
 │ 010 │ ⎮
 ├─────┤ ⎭
 │ 049 │
 ├─────┤
 │ 128 │  3
 ├─────┤
 │ 096 │ ⎫
 ├─────┤ ⎮
 │ 010 │ ⎬ 4
 ├─────┤ ⎮
 │ 049 │ ⎭
 └─────┘
```

The method used above to illustrate memory contents is one which you are going to see frequently in this book and in other books of this series. Memory is being likened to a ladder of *pigeon holes;* each pigeon hole represents an individually identifiable and addressable location.

Whenever a number is transferred from the CPU to memory, one pigeon hole will be filled. When a number is transferred from memory to the CPU, the CPU receives the contents of one pigeon hole.

Memory Locations and Addresses

Each pigeon hole is called a *memory location*. Every memory location is individually identifiable by a unique memory address.

We are not going to concern ourselves with how you create the memory address that identifies any individual addressable location within memory. Therefore, the addition program instruction sequence just illustrated will be represented occupying an undefined sequence of program memory locations as follows:

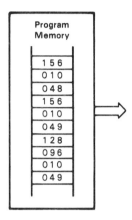

Without discussing memory addressing at all, we could illustrate the addition program instruction sequence occurring in the first ten addressable locations of program memory as follows:

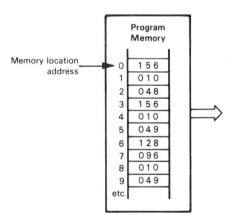

It takes no understanding of computer logic to see how the first ten addressable locations of program memory may be filled with numbers as illustrated above. It is going to take some understanding of computer logic in order to explain how we identify any one of these or any other memory location. This subject is discussed in Chapter 6.

Data Memory

The information which is used by a program while it executes is referred to as data. **In our simple addition example we are going to handle three pieces of data: the augend and the addend which are to be added, and the sum. These three piece of data will likely be stored in local, fast-access data memory.**

Addition Program Event Sequence

The process of adding two numbers may now be illustrated conceptually as follows:

Step 1: Fetch the Augend.

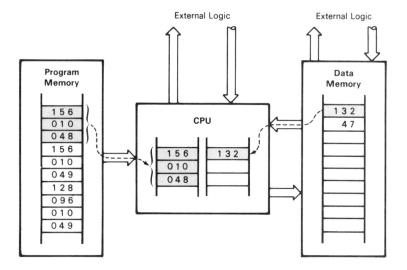

Step 2: Fetch the Addend.

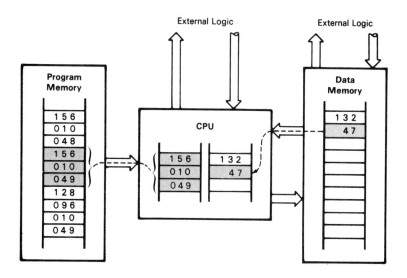

Step 3: Generate the Sum:

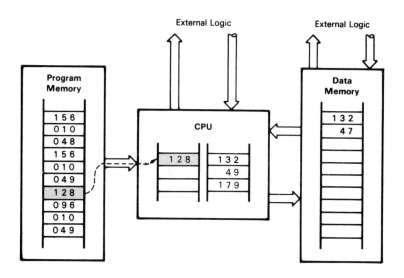

Step 4: Output the Sum.

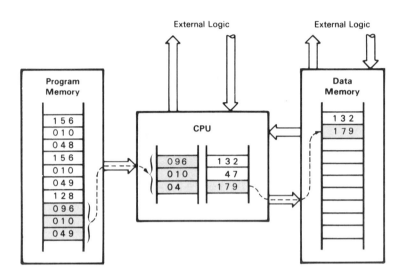

For each of the four steps illustrated above, the first event to occur will be the transfer of an instruction code from program memory to the CPU. In each step the instruction code is the shaded numbers in program memory. The CPU cannot know what to do until the instruction code has reached it. Once the instruction code has reached the CPU, operations required by the step actually occur. Operations are self-evident.

Note that in Step 4 the sum is arbitrarily shown being written back to the same data memory location from which the addend was fetched. Thus the addend will be lost.

6
Putting It All Together

We will now look at the logic of the Central Processing Unit itself. Chapter 5 superficially illustrated a CPU as follows:

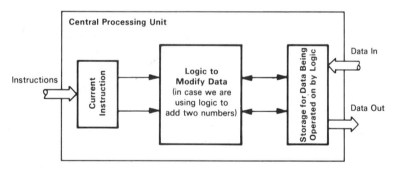

Word Size

In Chapter 4 we saw how instruction codes and data of various types all eventually become identical-looking bit patterns. Possibly the most important conceptual result of Chapter 4 is that although two-state switches, or bits, are not very useful on their own, groups of bits can be interpreted variously and powerfully. Therefore, **the first and most important decision a microprocessor designer has to make is to select**

the number of bits which the microprocessor will handle at one time. We call this number the microprocessor *word size*. You could design a microprocessor that uses as many bits as it needs at any given time, but no real microprocessors are designed that way. All real microprocessors have some fixed word size which applies to every type of information handled. Consider arithmetic; suppose the microprocessor is to add 4213_{10} and 246_{10}. This may be illustrated as follows:

Addition Example

Decimal		Binary			
		12 11 10 9 8 7 6 5 4 3 2 1 0	Bit Number
4 2 1 3		1 0 0 0 0 0 1 1 1 0 1 0 1	Augend
+ 2 4 6	+	1 1 1 1 0 1 1 0	Addend
4 4 5 9		1 0 0 0 1 0 1 1 0 1 0 1 1	Sum

The two numbers to be added require 13 bits for the augend, eight bits for the addend, and 13 bits for the sum. A microprocessor could conceivably be designed so that for the addition example illustrated above, it assigns 13 switches for the augend and the sum, and eight switches for the addend. But what happens if the very next addition requires seven switches for the augend, 15 switches for the addend, and 16 switches for the sum? Either the microprocessor must have some oversized switch set and waste a lot of switches most of the time,

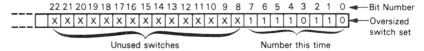

or the microprocessor must reuse the same switches in a variety of different ways, and that could become unbelievably complicated.

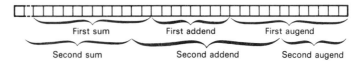

Fixed Bit Width   The type of complex logic illustrated above gives you no practical advantage over adopting some fixed bit width for all information handling. Consider eight bits (remember, eight bits is referred to as a byte). Our addition example would be implemented in byte units as follows:

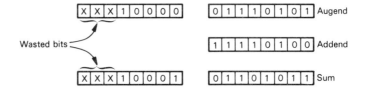

There are some wasted bits, but the simplified logic is more than enough compensation.

Most of the popular microprocessors on the market today handle information in 8-bit units. Consequently, these microprocessors are referred to as 8-bit machines. **A few obsolete microprocessors handle information in 4-bit units, while some of the newer, more powerful microprocessors handle information in 16-bit units.** Notice that these bit lengths — 4, 8, and 16 — are all designed to allow easy counting within a binary system.

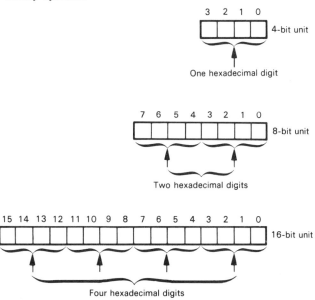

Let's look at the implications of a fixed word length. For an 8-bit microcomputer, all information — data, characters, and instruction codes — must be stored in units of eight binary digits. We are going to represent this 8-bit unit as follows:

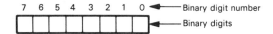

Buses

Information must also be transmitted from one part of a microcomputer system to another. Since all information is handled as 8-bit

units, all information transfers must occur eight bits at a time. These transfers, therefore, occur via eight parallel conductors.

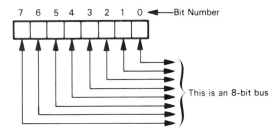

0 Bits and 1 Bits   **We call the conductors *buses*.** A *bus* is nothing more than a collection of electrical conducting lines over which binary data is transferred. A 1 bit or on switch is represented by the presence of voltage on the conductor; a 0 bit or off switch is represented by the absence of any voltage on the conductor. This may be illustrated as follows:

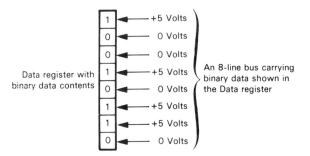

Representing Bus Line Signals

In order to identify signal levels on bus lines, we resort to a shorthand. For a single bus line we draw a continuous line; the line is high when voltage is present and it is low when no voltage is present. This may be illustrated as follows:

When a bus has more than one line, some lines may have voltage present while others do not. We identify the instant at which one or more bus lines change state as follows:

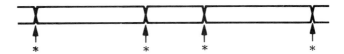

* One or more bus lines may change state at these points

Sometimes one signal's change in state triggers anothers signal's change in state. This "triggering" action is represented as follows:

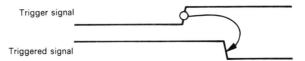

There is no significance to either signal change level; low-to-high ⌐ could be substituted for high-to-low ⌐, and vice versa. What is important is that one signal level change, as shown below,

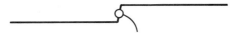

is identified as causing another signal to change state, as follows:

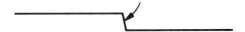

Registers

The switches that hold information are called *registers*. Information is transmitted to and from registers via buses. Now we can immediately see that a 4-bit microprocessor will be simpler than an 8-bit microprocessor, since every register or bus requires only four switches or conducting lines, rather than eight. Similarly, a 16-bit microprocessor has more complicated logic than an 8-bit microprocessor, because every register or bus requires 16 switches or conducting lines, rather than eight.

The Arithmetic and Logic Unit

A microprocessor's word size also applies to logic that handles data manipulations. All the various arithmetic and logic operations described in Chapter 4 will be performed on fixed bit length data units, equal to the word size of the microprocessor. Thus, for an 8-bit microprocessor you will always have 8-bit inputs to any arithmetic or Boolean operation, and you will create an 8-bit result. **All of this logic is collected together in one location which is referred to as an**

ALU ***Arithmetic and Logic Unit* (ALU).** The Arithmetic and Logic Unit gets its name from the fact that it performs arithmetic operations (addition and subtraction) and logic operations; principal logic operations are the Boolean operations AND, OR, XOR, and NOT. Figure 6-1 functionally illustrates the logic of an Arithmetic and Logic Unit.

In addition to performing the arithmetic and Boolean operations described in Chapter 4, an ALU will probably be able to shift data left,

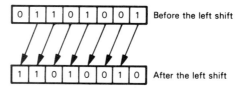

or it will be able to shift data right,

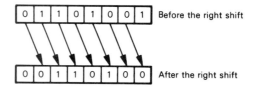

or both.

The 0 and 1 bits shown in the shift illustrations have been selected arbitrarily and have no particular significance.

We are not going to concern ourselves with the actual method used to create addition logic, or any other logic within the ALU. Only someone who is actually designing microprocessors needs this type of detail. What is worth noting is that the ALU has one or more buses bringing it data input, and one or more buses by which data is transmitted out. (The ALU will probably have one or more internal buses, as shown in Figure 6-1, but these are of no concern to you.) Buses become

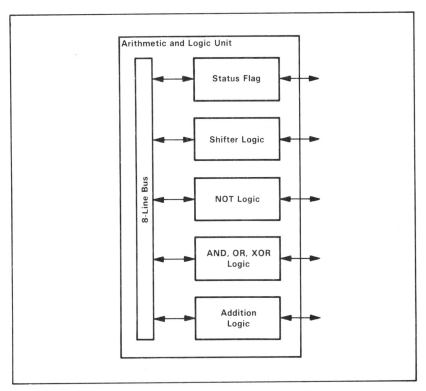

Figure 6-1. The Arithmetic and Logic Unit

4-bit buses for a 4-bit microprocessor, 8-bit buses for an 8-bit microprocessor, and 16-bit buses for a 16-bit microprocessor.

The only important aspect of Figure 6-1 is the fact that an ALU must be present to perform the actual data manipulations that may be required. For these data manipulations to occur, data must be transferred from data registers, via appropriate buses, to the ALU. The results of any data manipulations must be transferred via an appropriate bus back to a data register. Thus, the only "magic" that remains unexplained in any computer operation is the actual procedure whereby operations within the ALU occur. We are not going to describe internal ALU logic since there are probably as many ways of accomplishing the task as there are logic designers. Furthermore, to you as a microprocessor user, the subject is of no interest. But remember, no matter how complicated a computer operation you want to perform, it will ultimately be broken down into a sequence of steps, each of which involves sending binary data input to the ALU and receiving binary data results from the ALU.

Since the ALU receives operands from data registers and returns results to data registers, we must add appropriate data registers on one side of the ALU.

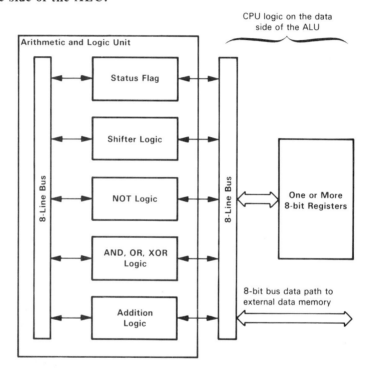

Control Unit   On the other side of the ALU we need a register which holds the instruction that determines which part of the ALU will be used, and how it will be used. The "which" and "how" determination is made by a new block of logic which we will call the *control unit*. This is shown on the following page.

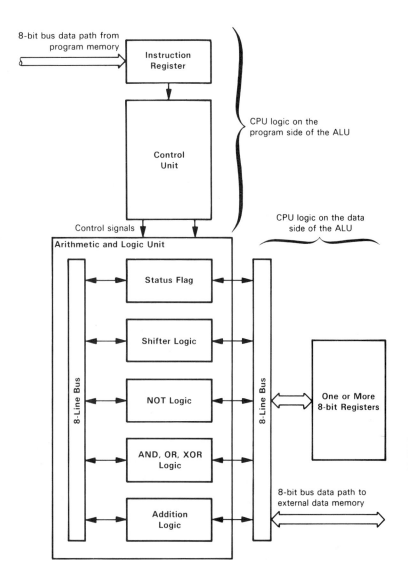

Additional CPU Logic

Let us now look at the logic on each side of the ALU.

Data Registers

Operands **On the data side of the ALU we need one or more registers to hold data that is being operated on by the ALU. There is no "common sense" number of data registers that every designer will include on the data side of the ALU. You might, for example, assume that three registers is a good idea,** because many arithmetic and Boolean operations use two operands and create one result.

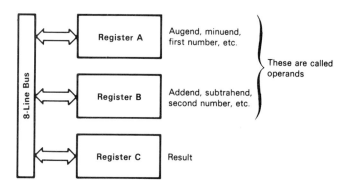

But by breaking up the arithmetic or Boolean operation into a number of steps, **you could get by with just one data register.** The following are the necessary steps:

1. Bring the first operand to the data register.

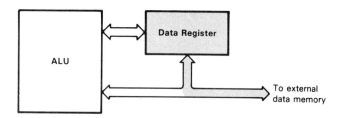

2. Perform any ALU operations, fetching one operand from the data register, the other operand directly from external memory.

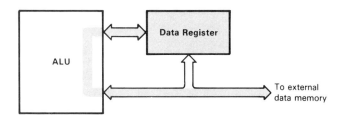

3. Return the result to the data register.

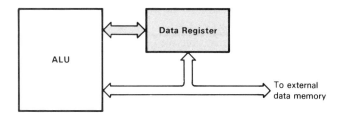

But **there are also good arguments for having more than three data registers** on the data side of the ALU. Data can be transferred between a register and the ALU much faster than between external data memory and the ALU. This is because there are very few data registers in the CPU, so you can immediately identify the register that is going to be accessed. There are a large number of external data memory locations, which means that every time the CPU accesses an external data memory location, there will be a whole memory location identification step involved (that is to say, CPU logic must spend time figuring out exactly which data memory location it is supposed to access). This may be illustrated as follows:

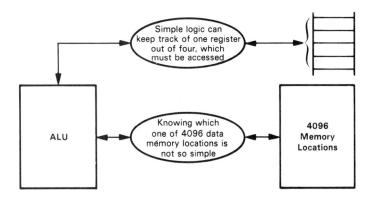

Using Data Registers

By having many data registers, a microprocessor allows you to maintain within the CPU any data which you are going to access frequently. To decide on the optimal number of data registers for a CPU, we need to have some understanding of the function data registers serve. We will, therefore, depart from our immediate discussion in order to look at a real example of how data registers are used.

In Susan Kilobyte's bill-paying program, whenever Susan enters a character via the keyboard, the program tests the character to see if it is an *Escape* or a *Carriage Return.* Some microcomputers do not have a "test" instruction; lacking test instructions, **you perform a test by subtracting the incoming character code from the** *Escape* **character, and then from the** *Carriage Return* **character.** Logic may be illustrated as follows:

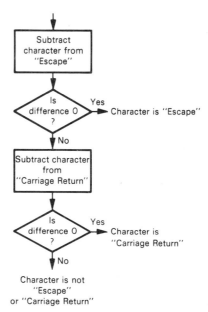

We will represent a Carriage Return keyboard character using the symbol <CR>. Does it make sense to subtract a letter of the alphabet from a Carriage Return?

$$<CR> - A = ?$$

Multiple Interpretations of Binary Data

To a human, this subtraction makes no sense; but remember, microcomputers represent characters via binary digit patterns — and they also represent numbers via binary digit patterns. Do you recall how frequently you were told in Chapter 4 that you must remember how a binary digit pattern is interpreted? Now we see that this has its advantages, as well as giving you more to remember. Suppose Susan Kilobyte presses the A key at her keyboard. The microcomputer sees the following binary digit pattern arrive from the keyboard:

0 1 0 0 0 0 0 1

This bit pattern will arrive on an 8-line bus, as follows:

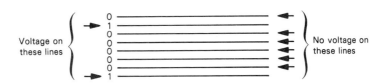

As far as the microcomputer is concerned, this is a simple binary digit pattern. If you preserve it in memory and reuse it later, you could send it out to a video display in order to echo the A; the video display has been designed to interpret all incoming bit patterns as ASCII characters. But within the CPU, a bit pattern is simply a bit pattern. Thus, you can subtract the A bit pattern from the Carriage Return bit pattern, treating each as pure binary data. This may be illustrated as follows:

$$
\begin{array}{ll}
<CR> & 0\,0\,0\,0\,1\,1\,0\,1 \\
-\ A & -\,0\,1\,0\,0\,0\,0\,0\,1 \\
\hline
CC_{16} & 1\,1\,0\,0\,1\,1\,0\,0
\end{array}
$$

ASCII character code

As long as you do not write anything into the registers holding the A or <CR> characters, the contents of the registers will be preserved. The next time you access these same registers, you can interpret the contents as ASCII characters. For example, you could transmit the A character code to the video display to generate an echo right after subtracting the A character code from a Carriage Return. We can now represent the whole instruction sequence which receives and tests incoming characters using a more complete flowchart (see Appendix C).

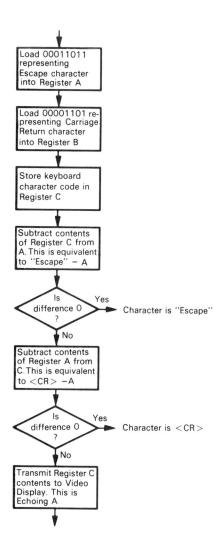

Zero
Status
Flag Following each subtraction, you will use a status flag in order to determine if the character is a Carriage Return or an Escape code. Nearly all microprocessors have a status flag called the zero status. This flag is used to detect zero results as follows:

> If result is 0, zero status flag is 1.
> If result is not 0, zero status flag is 0.

By a perverse twist of logic, the zero status flag is always set to 1 for a zero result and is set to 0 for a nonzero result. Now we can create our character-testing logic using the following instruction sequence:

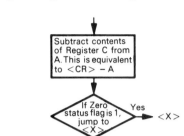

The instruction to be executed if a Carriage Return rather than an A is entered from the keyboard is <X>. You select this instruction and identify it by its program memory address (the address of the program memory location where the instruction code is stored).

All of this has been something of a departure from the discussion at hand — the correct number of registers to have on the data side of the ALU. But now that we understand how data registers are used, can we justify some "correct" number of data registers which every microprocessor should have? Unfortunately, there is no "correct" number. The microprocessor designer has to make trade-offs. How much of the limited logic is he or she going to set aside for registers and how much for other things? Remember, it takes eight switches for each register, plus connections from the register to buses within the microprocessor. The same switches and bus space could be used in a variety of other ways.

CPU
Memory

You will commonly find between four and eight registers on the data side of the ALU, although you may have as few as one register and as many as 32. There are also some microprocessors that have a small part of data memory within the CPU. There may be 64 or more data memory locations within the CPU. These storage locations are something more than external data memory locations, yet something less than true data registers.

The Instruction Register and Control Unit

On the program memory side of the ALU, there must be a single register within which we can hold the binary code representing the instruction currently being executed. We refer to this as the _instruction register_.

Suppose the instruction currently being executed adds the contents of data registers A and B, returning the sum to data register A. (We assume for the moment that data registers A and B exist on the data side of the CPU.) The appropriate binary instruction code will be brought (as data) to the CPU, where it will be stored in the instruction register.

The contents of the instruction register act as one of 256 different "triggers" to a block of logic called the *control unit;* there are 256 different triggers because there are 256 combinations of 0 and 1 bits that you can generate out of eight bits. A 16-bit microprocessor would have a 16-bit instruction register — with 5536 different 0 and 1 bit combinations.

The instruction register trigger initiates a sequence of signals output by the control unit to enable the data transfers and ALU operations required by the instruction being executed.

There is very little you need to know about the control unit, the instruction register, and the way in which they interact; the control unit creates control signals that move data where it is supposed to be moved and exercise ALU logic at the proper time. For microcomputers currently on the market, there is nothing that you, as a microcomputer user, can do about the control unit; you cannot, for example, modify the way in which it responds to an instruction code. The control unit acts as the link between an instruction and the events which occur when the instruction is executed. That is all you need to know about the control unit.

But the size of the instruction register is important. An 8-bit instruction register can only specify 256 different operations and variations on operations. That is because there are only 256 different patterns of 0 and 1 digits that you can create out of eight binary digits. This may seem like a large number, but in reality it is not. **Consider Arithmetic and Logic Unit operations.** Within this block of logic we have defined just seven operations.

Shift left
Shift right
Complement
AND
OR
Exclusive-OR
Add

Even though there are only seven ALU operations, the instruction has much more to define: it must define the sources for the operands, and the destination for the result. Suppose you have four data registers (registers A, B, C, and D). You will need two of the eight instruction object code bits each time you have to identify one of the four registers.

0 0 Select Register A
0 1 Select Register B
1 0 Select Register C
1 1 Select Register D

In other words, an instruction code must be absolutely specific. If you have four register options, you will need four separate and distinct binary digit codes to specify the selected option. **The 8-bit instruction code may be illustrated as follows:**

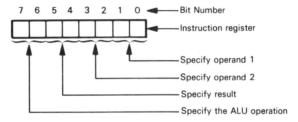

Bit Number
Instruction register
Specify operand 1
Specify operand 2
Specify result
Specify the ALU operation

We might arbitrarily assume that for each of the three register specifications, the control unit will interpret instruction code bits as follows:

00 - Select Data Register A
01 - Select Data Register B
10 - Select Data Register C
11 - Select Data Register D

Instruction register bits 6 and 7 might be interpreted by the control unit as follows:

Bits
7 6

0 0 Add
0 1 AND
1 0 OR
1 1 Exclusive-OR

The following is one example of how an instruction code would be interpreted:

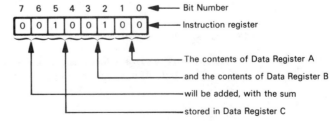

Bit Number
Instruction register
The contents of Data Register A
and the contents of Data Register B
will be added, with the sum
stored in Data Register C

We have accurately illustrated the way in which the control unit decodes instruction register contents, but the illustration, while conceptually accurate, is impractical.

The bit patterns just illustrated apply to only four of the seven ALU operations — the four that require two input operands. But these four operations, together with their options, use all 256 instruction codes. There are no codes left for any other ALU operations, nor for any of the instructions that do not use the ALU. Clearly, 256 possible instruction combinations is not very many. In *Volume 1* we will explore the ways in which microprocessor designers spread the limited number of instruction code options among all the types of instructions which must be present, giving a limited capability within each class of instructions. This is a process anyone can understand, since it's about the same as getting by on a limited budget. You don't have enough money to do everything you'd like, so you limit yourself in all areas, striking the best balance between lifestyle and income.

Logic Concepts and Timing

Even though the exact workings of a control unit are unimportant to you, there are some logic concepts which are important because they apply universally within microcomputer systems. We will now look at these concepts.

Any sequence of logic operations within the CPU (or any other part of a microcomputer system) will consist of moving and changing binary data.

Within the CPU, binary data must be moved between data registers, the ALU, and external logic. Binary data is changed only within the ALU.

In any other part of a microcomputer system, binary data will be moved between registers and the data will be modified by logic that is simpler than, but similar to, the ALU.

Logic to Move Binary Data

Gate Signal   **In order to move binary data, a control signal must be created to act as a connector** between a register switch and a bus line. This control signal is sometimes referred to as a *gate*. You may gate data from bus lines into a register.

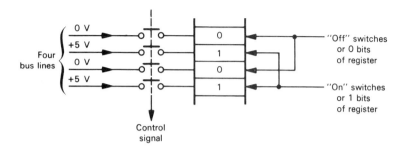

The switch position (or register bit) may be gated onto a bus line.

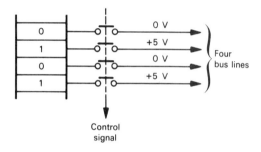

Instruction Timing

Timing is extremely important during these data transfer operations because it takes a finite amount of time for voltage levels to appear or disappear on bus lines; and until a steady state exists on the bus line, logic cannot connect the bus lines to any new switch. Also, the sequence of events corresponding to any instruction's execution must occur in some very specific order. Consider our addition example; the necessary event sequence within the CPU is shown on the following pages.

Step 1. Bring the instruction code into the instruction register.

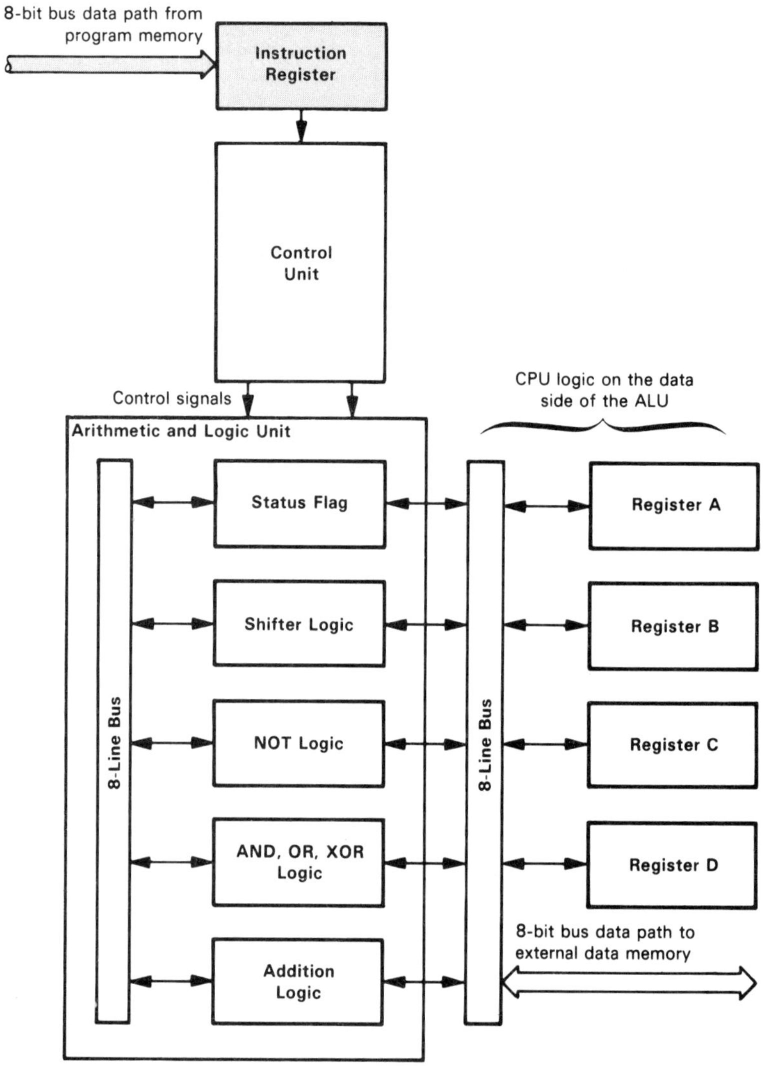

8-bit bus data path from
program memory

Instruction Register

Control Unit

Control signals

CPU logic on the data side of the ALU

Arithmetic and Logic Unit

8-Line Bus

8-Line Bus

| **Status Flag** | **Register A** |

| **Shifter Logic** | **Register B** |

| **NOT Logic** | **Register C** |

| **AND, OR, XOR Logic** | **Register D** |

| **Addition Logic** |

8-bit bus data path to
external data memory

Step 2. Gate Register A contents onto the bus.

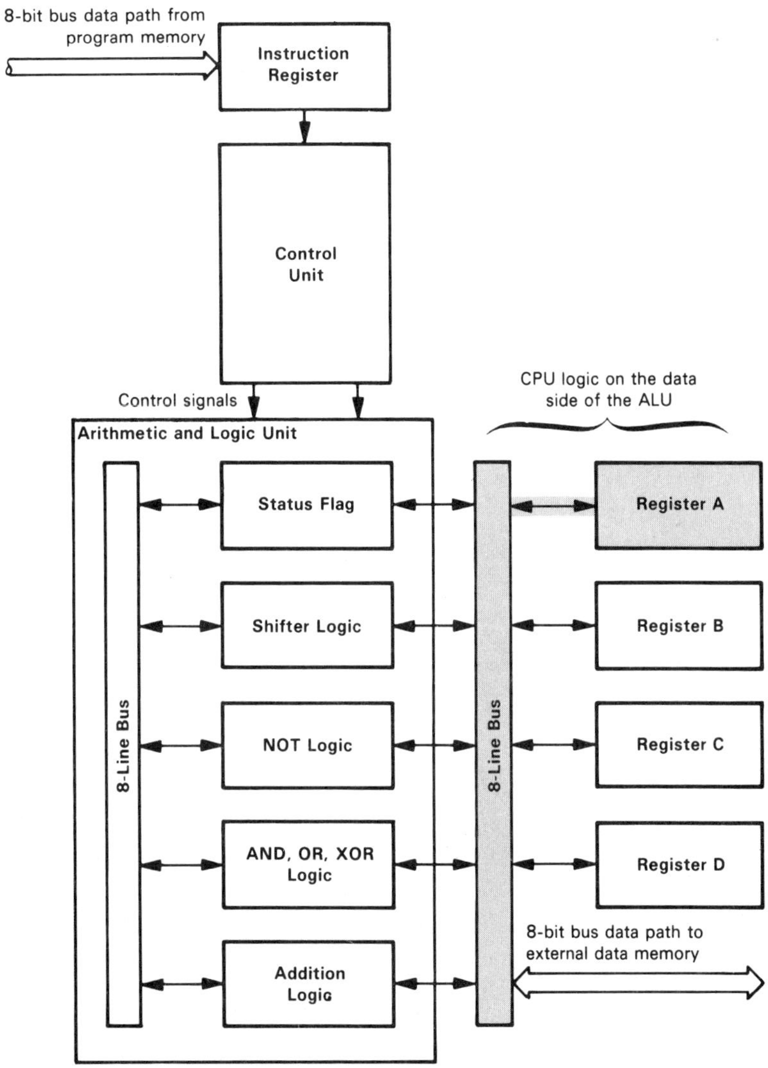

8-bit bus data path from
program memory

Instruction
Register

Control
Unit

CPU logic on the data
side of the ALU

Control signals

Arithmetic and Logic Unit

Status Flag

Register A

Shifter Logic

Register B

8-Line Bus

NOT Logic

8-Line Bus

Register C

AND, OR, XOR
Logic

Register D

8-bit bus data path to
external data memory

Addition
Logic

Step 3. Gate bus to Addition logic.

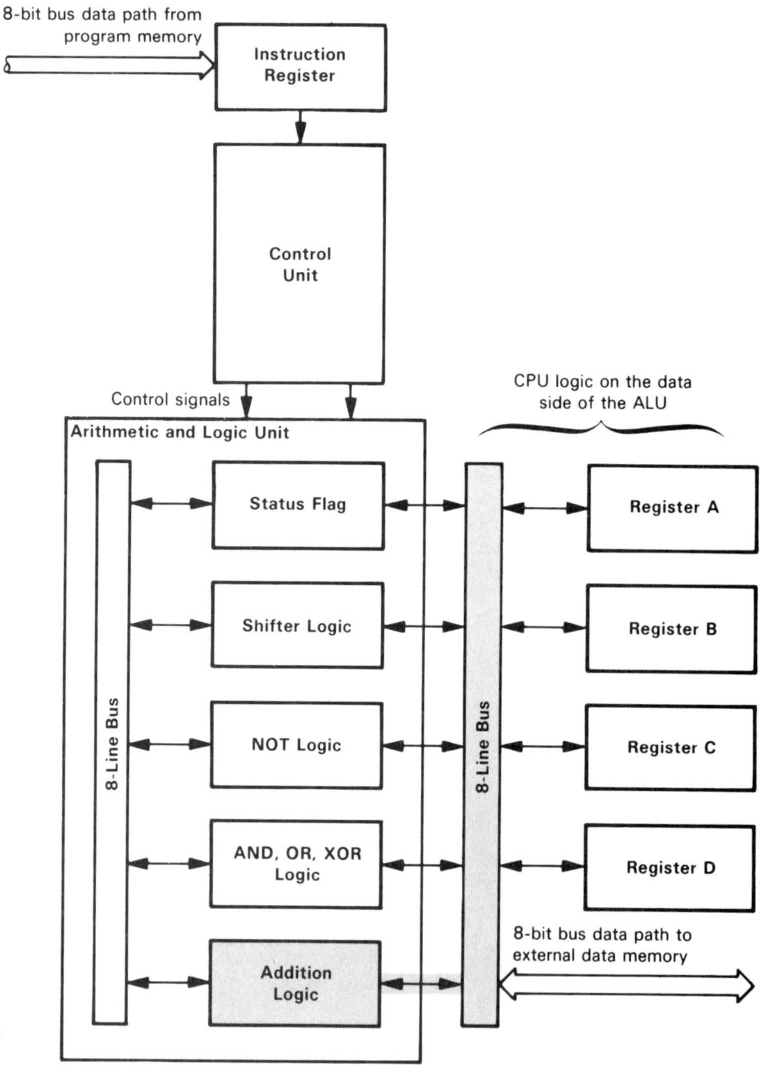

8-bit bus data path from
program memory

Instruction
Register

Control
Unit

Control signals

CPU logic on the data
side of the ALU

Arithmetic and Logic Unit

8-Line Bus

Status Flag

Shifter Logic

NOT Logic

AND, OR, XOR
Logic

Addition
Logic

8-Line Bus

Register A

Register B

Register C

Register D

8-bit bus data path to
external data memory

Step 4. Gate Register B contents onto the bus.

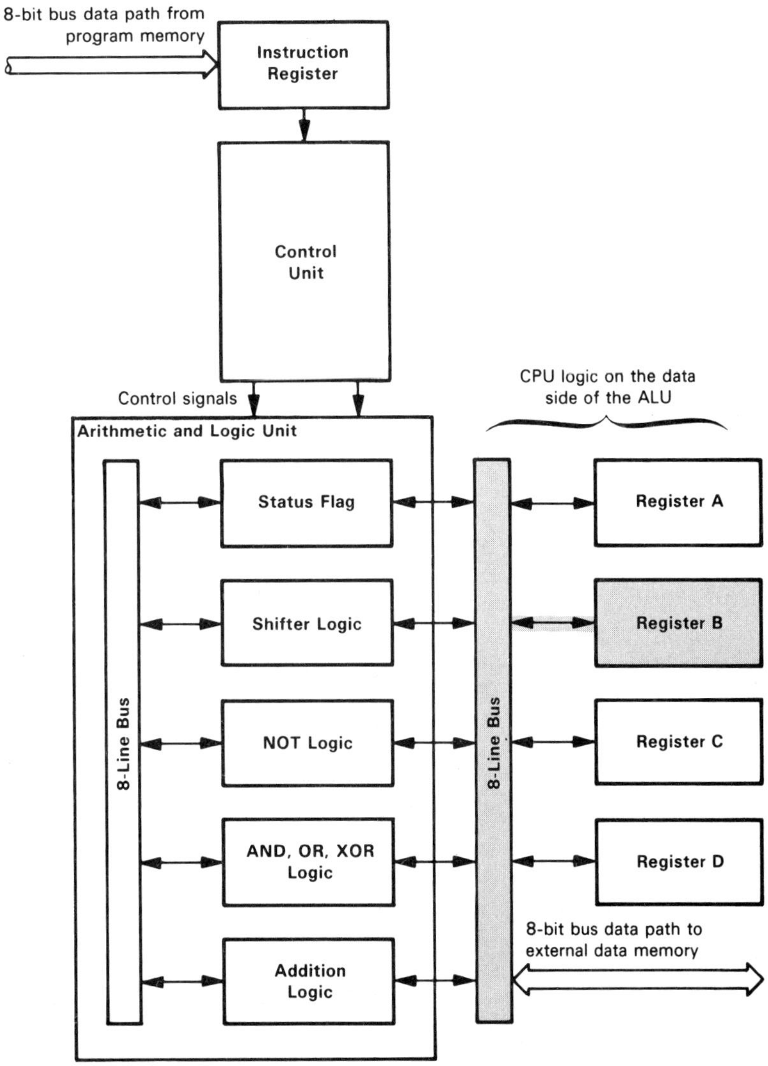

8-bit bus data path from
program memory

```
Instruction
Register
```

```
Control
Unit
```

CPU logic on the data
side of the ALU

Control signals

Arithmetic and Logic Unit

Status Flag	Register A
Shifter Logic	**Register B**
NOT Logic	Register C
AND, OR, XOR Logic	Register D
Addition Logic	

8-Line Bus

8-Line Bus

8-bit bus data path to
external data memory

Step 5. Add.

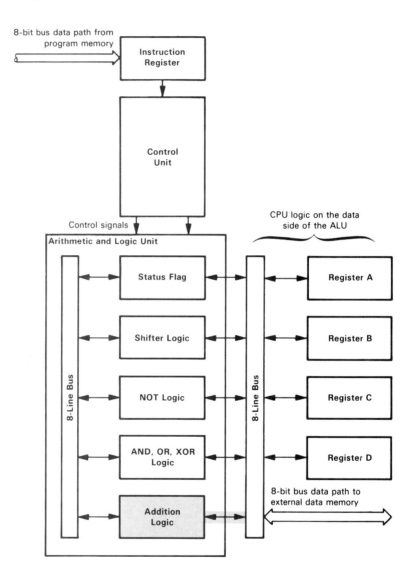

Step 6. Gate sum onto the bus.

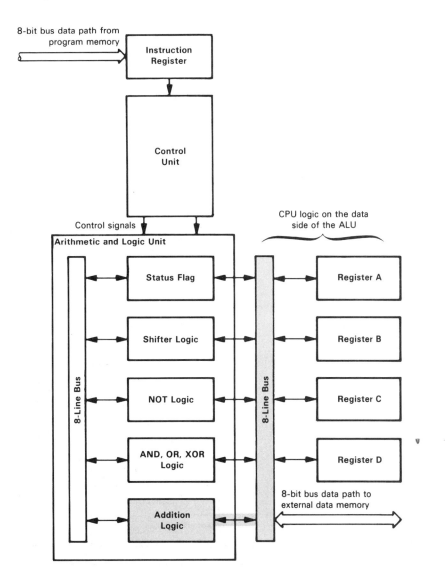

Step 7. Gate sum into Register C.

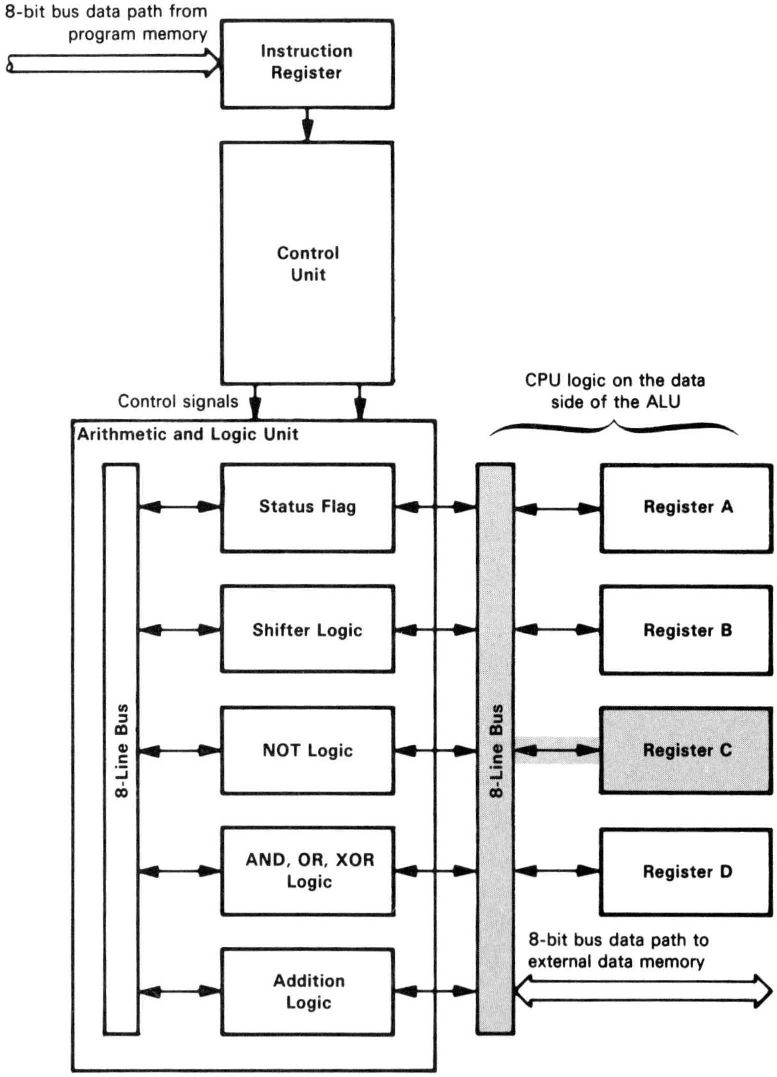

8-bit bus data path from
program memory

**Instruction
Register**

**Control
Unit**

Control signals

CPU logic on the data
side of the ALU

Arithmetic and Logic Unit

8-Line Bus

8-Line Bus

Status Flag

Register A

Shifter Logic

Register B

NOT Logic

Register C

**AND, OR, XOR
Logic**

Register D

8-bit bus data path to
external data memory

**Addition
Logic**

The Clock Signal and
Instruction Execution Timing

Event sequences such as the seven steps just illustrated are scheduled by a *clock signal,* so named because it generates regular, periodic voltage pulses. A clock signal may be illustrated as follows:

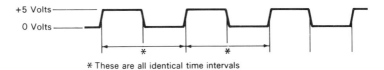

* These are all identical time intervals

The clock signal illustrated above is shown switching between 0 volts and +5 volts. While these voltage levels are commonly seen in microcomputer circuits, there is no intrinsic reason why they should be selected. The logical necessities of chip design demand that two voltages be used to represent 0 and 1 binary digit levels. Functionally, it makes no difference what voltages are selected. Older micro-processors use more than two voltage levels. Additional voltage levels simply make the job of designing the chip easier; they play no part in representing 0 or 1 binary digits.

Leading Edge   **The transition from no voltage to some voltage is referred to as the *leading edge* of a clock signal.**

Trailing Edge   **The transition from voltage to no voltage is referred to as the *trailing edge* of a clock signal.**

All signals have leading and trailing edges, not just clock signals.

The leading and/or trailing edges of the clock signal are used to time events within the CPU and throughout the microcomputer system. For our additional example, this may be illustrated concep-tually as follows:

Step 1   Step 2   Step 3   Step 4   Step 5   Step 6   Step 7

More time follows Step 1 than any other step since the control unit must be given time to decode the instruction register contents.

Different microcomputers have different types of clock signals, ranging from the very simple to the very complex. There may also be more than one clock signal, in which case the many clock signals will have some definite relationship to each other. But **in every case it is the clock signal that acts as the master event sequencer for all logic.**

Instruction Fetch

Let us look again at an instruction execution's event sequence. **Every instruction's execution must begin with a step that brings the binary instruction code from program memory to the instruction register. We call this step an** *instruction fetch.* Once the binary instruction code is in the instruction register the control unit takes over —after being triggered appropriately by the instruction register. The control unit acquires as much time as it needs in order to generate the logic events required by the instruction. After all logic events have been completed, the control unit initiates the next instruction fetch. Thus, **every instruction's execution may be divided into an instruction fetch phase and an instruction execute phase. This is illustrated as follows:**

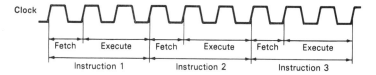

The instruction fetch phase will take the same amount of time for every instruction, but the instruction execute phase will require different amounts of time for different instructions. Some microprocessors have variable instruction execution times, but in order to simplify logic, other microprocessors use one, or a very few, fixed instruction execution times. **Suppose, for example, different instructions require execution phases lasting one, two, three, or four clock pulses.** If the instruction fetch phase lasts one clock pulse, then we could design the microprocessor to execute instructions in two, three, four, or five pulses.

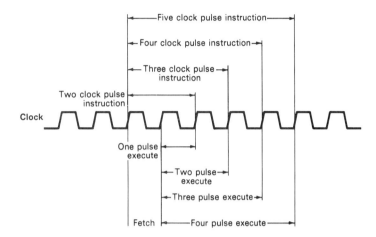

Given the above situation, **a microprocessor designer may decide to make all instructions last five clock pulses,** wasting the unused clock pulses for the shorter instructions. If, on the other hand, there were very few long instructions, **the microprocessor designer could decide to standardize a four-clock-pulse instruction time, using two instruction times for the new five-clock-pulse instructions.** This may be illustrated as follows:

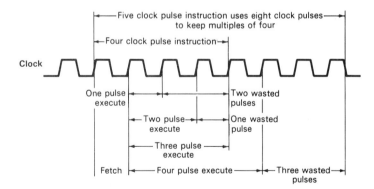

Machine   **In the illustration above, four clock pulses constitute** an important
Cycle   control unit time interval, **the basic time unit for all instruction executions. This time unit is frequently called a *machine cycle.*** Not all microprocessors use a fixed time interval machine cycle to time instruction executions, but for those that do, all instructions will execute in some fixed number of machine cycles — usually one machine cycle, but sometimes two or three.

Clock Signal Frequency

But all instructions are executed in some fixed number of clock pulses. **Therefore, the speed with which your microcomputer executes programs will vary linearly with the speed of your clock signal.**

A clock signal's speed is also referred to as the clock signal frequency. Clock signal frequency may be illustrated as follows:

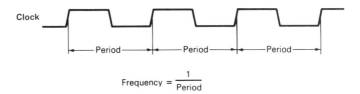

$$\text{Frequency} = \frac{1}{\text{Period}}$$

Clock Period

Nanosecond

Microsecond

Megahertz

The clock period is the time that elapses between repeated identical clock wave shapes. Clock periods are measured in nanoseconds. One nanosecond is equal to one-thousandth of one-millionth of one second (1×10^{-9} seconds). **The period of a clock signal will vary between 100 nanoseconds and 500 nanoseconds.** A few microprocessors use a clock signal of one microsecond. One microsecond is equal to one-millionth of a second.

The frequency of a clock signal is called the reciprocal of the clock period; that means it is equal to one second divided by the clock period. If the period is one microsecond, the frequency will be 1 million pulses per second. **A clock signal with 1 million pulses per second is referred to as a 1 megahertz (MHz) clock signal.** A clock signal with a period of 500 nanoseconds will have 2 million pulses per second.

$$\frac{1}{500 \times 10^{-9}} = \frac{1}{5 \times 10^{-7}} = \frac{10,000,000}{5} = 2\,000\,000$$

Therefore, this clock signal is referred to as a 2 megahertz (2 MHz) clock signal. A clock signal with a period of 100 nanoseconds will generate 10 million pulses per second.

$$\frac{1}{100 \times 10^{-9}} = \frac{1}{1 \times 10^{-7}} = 10\,000\,000$$

This clock signal is said to have a frequency of 10 megahertz (10 MHz).

Memory Access

Nothing can happen within a microcomputer system before a memory access occurs. Every instruction begins with an instruction fetch, which requires that the contents of some identifiable program memory location be fetched as data and loaded into the instruction register. Similarly, any data that is in a data register must be fetched either from an external physical unit, or from data memory. Likewise, the results of ALU operations in data registers must be sent back to data memory. **Since even a system with a small memory will have more than 1000 addressable locations, the method for identifying the single location that you wish to access is not immediately apparent.**

We showed earlier how it was possible to identify one of four data registers using two bits of the instruction code.

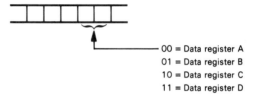

00 = Data register A
01 = Data register B
10 = Data register C
11 = Data register D

This easy method of addressing data registers, if applied to external memory, may have to address up to 65,536 memory locations; it takes a 16-binary-digit number to select one addressable location out of 65,536:

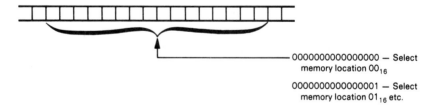

0000000000000000 — Select memory location 00_{16}

0000000000000001 — Select memory location 01_{16} etc.

Many microcomputers do allow you to directly address a memory location by supplying a 16-bit memory address; but this means the instruction is represented by three bytes of binary data, not one.

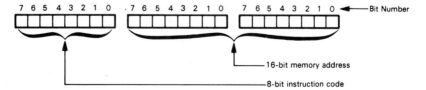

7 6 5 4 3 2 1 0   7 6 5 4 3 2 1 0   7 6 5 4 3 2 1 0 ◀— Bit Number

16-bit memory address

8-bit instruction code

But there are some problems associated with this approach to creating memory addresses.

In the first place, **it wastes memory.** Most microcomputers do not have 65,536 bytes of actual memory and since memory reference instructions occur frequently, alternative, more economical memory addressing procedures are needed. Furthermore, **even though we speak of program memory and data memory,** in most microcomputer systems **they are usually the same thing.**

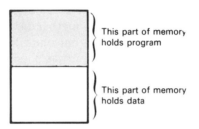

This part of memory holds program

This part of memory holds data

When you write a program for a microcomputer you decide which part of memory becomes program memory; the remainder of memory is data memory. But the next time you write a program, or if someone else writes a program for the microcomputer, **you may find memory allocated between the program and data areas in completely different ways.**

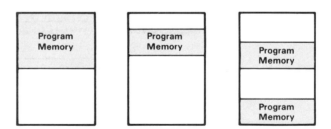

Frequently you will write simple programs, for example, to perform arithmetic on standard dollar amount numbers. The **programs will only be practical if you can reuse them in many applications. To do this you will need a memory addressing technique that identifies a data memory location in terms of its displacement (or distance) from the beginning of the data area of memory, rather than from the beginning of memory.**

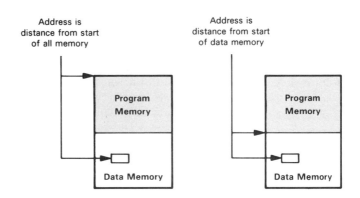

Let's look at the advantages of identifying a memory location by its displacement from the beginning of a data area. The most important advantage is that you can move the data area without having to change programs that access the data area. In order to understand why this is so, consider the everyday problem of identifying time. You can identify time by the time of day — which is equivalent to absolute memory addressing — or you can identify time as some number of hours before or after a movable event. This latter method is equivalent to addressing memory as a displacement from the beginning of the data area. Suppose you have to leave instructions for the preparation of dinner. Your instructions could state:

1. Turn the oven on at 6:00 p.m.
2. At 6:15 p.m. place the stew in the oven
3. Remove the stew at 8:15 p.m.
4. Serve at 8:30 p.m.

If you change dinner time, you must change all of your dinner preparation instructions. On the other hand, you could rewrite the dinner preparation instructions as follows:

1. Turn the oven on 2½ hours before dinner
2. At 2¼ hours before dinner, put the stew in the oven
3. Fifteen minutes before dinner, take the stew out of the oven
4. Serve dinner at dinner time.

Since these instructions address time as a displacement from dinner time, changing dinner time does not change dinner preparation instructions. Clearly, this is a more useful way of addressing time; it is equivalent to addressing memory by means of a displacement from the beginning of a data area.

Without exploring too many ideas for creating memory addressing, it is clear that a case can be made for having a variety of different memory addressing techniques.

Memory   Memory addressing describes, in general, the techniques that a
Addressing   microprocessor allows you to use in order to identify memory locations.

Memory Addressing Logic

Memory itself consists of logic devices that handle three types of information: addresses, data, and control signals.

Every memory access starts with an address being transmitted to the memory device.

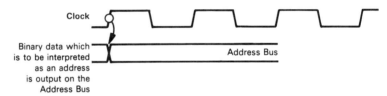

You will recall from our discussion earlier in this chapter that we use the shorthand

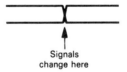

to identify the instant at which one or more signals on a multiline bus may change level. For a single signal we can show the actual change — from low to high

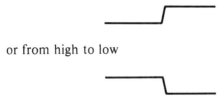

or from high to low

Address   A memory address consists of binary data being output on an
Bus   appropriate bus which we call **the *address bus*.** The address bus, like any other bus, is a number of parallel conductors connecting the CPU

to memory devices of the microcomputer system. This is illustrated in Figure 6-2.

Data Bus **There will be a separate** *data bus* connecting the Central Processing Unit to memory devices. The data bus is also illustrated in Figure 6-2. Once the CPU places binary data on a bus, there is no longer any possibility for errors in interpretation. Binary data appearing on the address bus must be interpreted as an address, while binary data appearing on the data bus must be interpreted as data.

Timing illustrations in this chapter show the address appearing on the address bus at the rising edge of a clock pulse. Logic within the CPU will use an appropriate rising clock pulse edge as the trigger to create control signals that connect address bus lines to a data register within the CPU. It is this connection which causes the data to become an address.

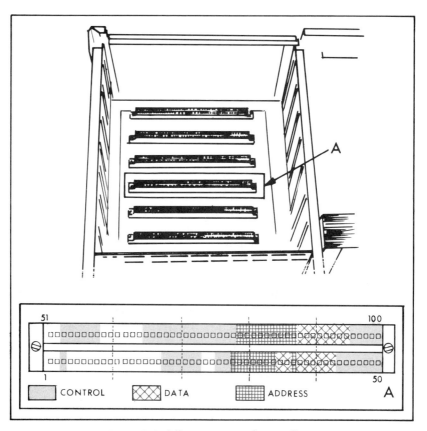

Figure 6-2. Microcomputer System Buses

Logic within the CPU will be able to connect the data bus and the address bus to the same data registers. This allows you to compute addresses, like any other data, before outputting the data as an address on the address bus. This may be illustrated as follows:

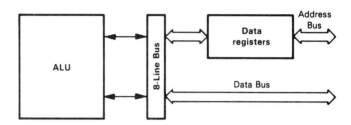

The important point to understand is that logic within the CPU can interpret binary data in any way. But once the data appears on a bus beyond the CPU, the bus upon which the data appears will, to a limited extent, determine how the data is to be interpreted. For example, information on the address bus must be a memory address, but this memory address can come from anywhere within the CPU, and external logic is only "supposed" to interpret it as an address. If external logic uses the address bus in some other way, CPU logic will not interfere.

Now look at the way in which the CPU and memory devices converse via bus lines.

Every memory location within a memory device will have a unique address assigned to it. The memory device decodes the binary data on the address bus and uses it to *select* a single memory location. Subsequently, data may be transmitted to the memory device via the data bus. In the case of a write operation, it will be stored in the selected memory location; for a read operation, data may be transmitted from the memory device, via the data bus, to the CPU. Control signals generated by the CPU determine whether the CPU reads data from memory or writes data to memory. Thus, **the connection between memory and the CPU will consist of an address bus, a data bus, and control signals. These are illustrated in Figure 6-2.**

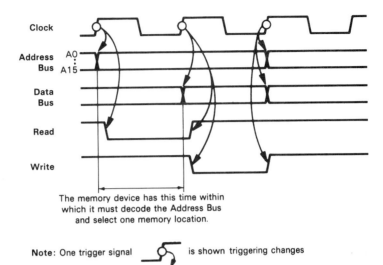

The memory device has this time within
which it must decode the Address Bus
and select one memory location.

Note: One trigger signal   is shown triggering changes

in more than one triggered signal level.

There are some important concepts embodied in the previous illustration.

Consider the address bus. It consists of 16 parallel lines — the most common size for microcomputer address buses. A 16-line address bus can carry a 16-bit address capable of addressing up to 65,536 different memory locations.

The address itself is shown being gated onto the address bus at the rising edge of a clock pulse. The address is maintained on the address bus for two clock pulses. During this time period, the CPU keeps the address bus lines connected to the data register bits out of which the address is being generated. We refer to this time period as the period during which the address is *stable* on the address bus.

Now look at the data bus. Once again there will be some period of time during which data on the data bus must be stable. This period will again be defined by clock signal edges. The data bus will start being stable at some time interval after the address bus is stable. This delay is necessary, since logic on the memory device must be given time to receive and respond to the address on the address bus. By the time the data is stable on the data bus, the addressed memory location has had time to become selected.

Memory Read Control If a memory read operation is to occur, the read control signal will be pulsed. A low pulse is arbitrarily illustrated; however, it could just as easily be a high pulse. In either case what is important is that the control signal has a *passive* state during which nothing happens and an *active* state during which it indicates something is happening — in this case a read operation is occurring.

A read operation requires that the addressed memory location contents be placed on the data bus. Once again we need an amount of time for logic at the memory device to sense the low read pulse and respond to it by placing data from the addressed memory location on the data bus. The low read pulse must, therefore, occur early enough to give memory logic time to transfer data from the selected memory location to the data bus. This may be illustrated as follows:

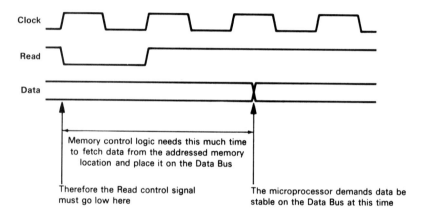

Memory Write Control   **The write control signal, which again is shown as a low pulse signal, indicates that data on the data bus is to be written into the addressed memory word.** The write control signal acts as a strobe; it cannot occur *true* (a low pulse is true) until valid data is stable on the data bus. This is because the memory device will use the low write strobe in order to connect the data bus to the addressed memory location. Were the low write strobe to occur in advance of stable data on the data bus, erroneous data might be written into the memory device.

Memory Read Operation   **Now let's look at memory read and write operations individually. The following is a timing diagram for a read operation.**

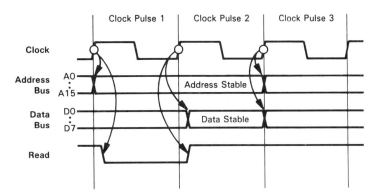

The memory read operation begins on the leading edge of clock pulse 1. The CPU uses this clock pulse to connect appropriate data registers to the address bus and this initiates a stable address appearing on the address bus:

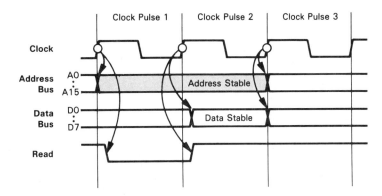

Shortly thereafter, the read control signal goes low.

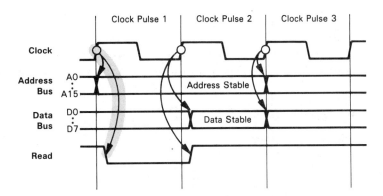

Memory logic decodes the contents of the address bus in order to identify a single memory location as *selected.* This memory location select logic is nothing more than a combination of Boolean operations performed on the individual signals of the address bus. However, the actual method used by a memory device to decode the contents of the address bus is not important, as long as you realize that logic exists to select one single memory location out of 65,536 possibilities. The accompanying read control signal causes the memory device to connect the bits of the selected memory location to the data bus. The process of identifying a single memory location, and then connecting it with a data bus, must occur before the leading edge of clock pulse 2.

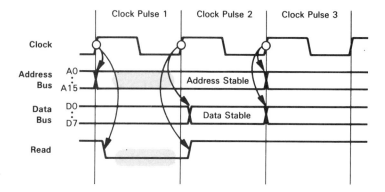

At this time the contents of the selected memory location must be stable on the data bus. This data must be held stable on the data bus for a finite amount of time: the amount of time the CPU must be given in order to get the data off the data bus and load it into an appropriate data register.

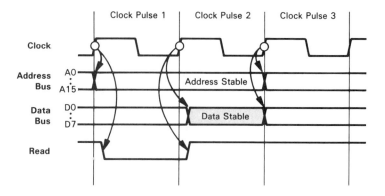

The CPU connects the appropriate data register to the data bus and the read is completed.

In the previous illustrations, one clock pulse is shown as the time duration during which the data on the data bus is held stable.

Now consider a memory write operation. Its timing may be illustrated as follows:

**Memory
Write
Operation**

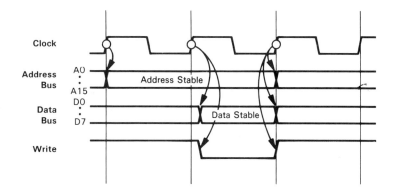

Timing associated with a memory write operation does not differ significantly from timing associated with a memory read operation. The logic that outputs a stable address on the address bus is identical for the two operations. Differences occur on the data bus and the control signals. When the address appears on the address bus, there is no accompanying low write control signal; therefore, the selected memory location is not connected to the data bus and its contents are not output on the data bus. Subsequently, the CPU connects an appropriate data register to the data bus in order to output stable data.

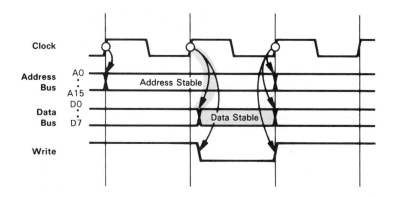

At this time the write control signal is pulsed low. The write control signal will be received by the memory device and used to connect the selected memory location to the data bus so that the contents of the data bus are written into the selected memory location and permanently stored.

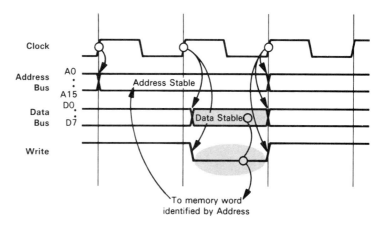

Program Memory Addressing and The Program Counter

Let us now look at the CPU registers that are required in order to create memory addresses. We will begin by looking at program memory addressing.

Logic required to address program memory is quite straightforward. A program is nothing more than a sequence of instruction codes that will normally be stored in memory locations with incrementing addresses.

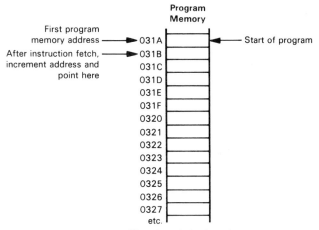

These hexadecimal numbers
have been arbitrarily selected to represent
instruction codes.

**Program
Counter**

This being the case, all we need to do is identify the address of the first instruction within the sequence. After every instruction fetch, if we increment this address, it will accurately point to the next instruction in the sequence. This program memory addressing logic is handled by a register referred to as a *program counter.* The program counter contains binary data that is interpreted as a memory address because the binary data is output on to the address bus. Thus the program counter provides the memory address for all instruction fetch operations; to external memory an instruction fetch looks exactly like any memory read operation. This is illustrated on the following page.

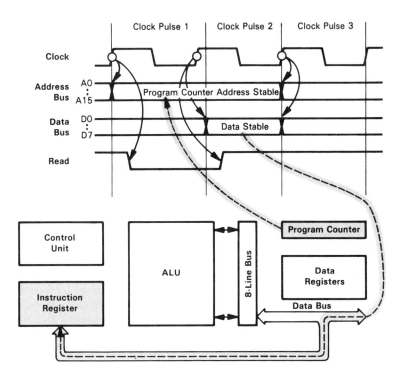

Program Logic and the Program Counter

The program counter is treated within the CPU logic both as an address generation register and as a data register. It is very important that the program counter be accessible as a data register because this is the basis for program logic.

We have already seen in program flowcharts the decision-making steps that allow the program to continue by executing the next sequential instruction or some out-of-sequence instruction.

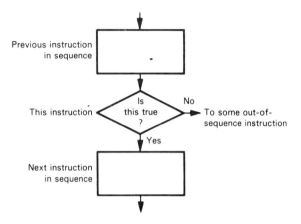

Jump Instruction   How do we identify and then fetch an out-of-sequence instruction? The answer is by knowing in advance the address of this out-of-sequence instruction. If we load this known address, as data, into the program counter, we execute a jump instruction. When the jump instruction is executed, the program counter is pointing to the jump instruction itself.

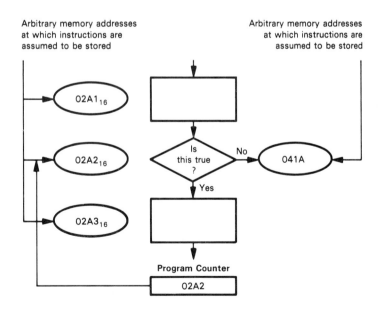

After the jump instruction has been fetched, the program counter will be left pointing to the next sequential instruction.

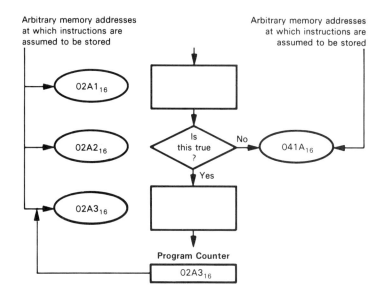

If the jump is to occur, then the CPU will make the jump happen by loading the out-of-sequence instruction's address, as data, into the program counter. This data is loaded into the program counter during the instruction execute phase of the jump instruction.

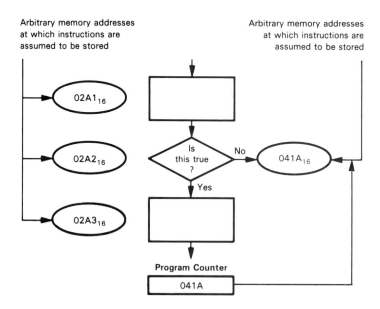

Now when the jump instruction has finished executing, and the next instruction starts executing, an instruction fetch will occur; but instead of getting the next sequential instruction, you get the new out-of-sequence instruction.

Data Memory Addressing Registers

As we saw earlier in this chapter, addressing data memory is not as straightforward as addressing program memory, because there is no "usual" sequence in which data will be stored. Thus, a variety of ingenious techniques are used to create addresses for data memory.

Data memory address computation becomes a simple extension of logic on the data side of the Arithmetic and Logic Unit. Given data registers in which we can store binary data, plus an ALU that we can use to perform computations, we have all the prerequisites to calculate binary data that will subsequently become data memory addresses. Thus, data memory address computation is easily handled by logic already present in a CPU.

In this book we are going to discuss the various methods used to create data memory addresses. This is information that becomes necessary when you start learning how to write programs in assembly language, and that is material for *Volume 1*. A data memory address is the result of data computations that preceded a data access; that is all you need to understand for now.

External Logic Addressing

In order to access some external logic or peripheral device (such as a keyboard or video display), the CPU will go through a sequence of steps that are very similar to those required to access memory. The actual external logic device being accessed will have a specific address, just as every memory location has a specific address. Thus, **accessing the external device consists of the following steps:**

1. Generate an I/O device address (this address is a binary number which is created as data and then output on an address bus).

2. Trigger appropriate control signals that tell the I/O device what to do.

3. Transmit or receive data via a data bus.

The event sequence associated with accessing external logic or I/O

devices is so similar to a memory reference that many micro-processors treat them as the same thing. In this case, I/O devices and external logic respond to exactly the same signals as a memory device, and the only thing that separates the two is the memory addresses that are set aside for each.

Microprocessors that treat memory and I/O devices separately have, in effect, a secondary set of logic that duplicates memory addressing logic — but on a smaller scale. For example, where the address bus for memory commonly consists of 16 lines capable of addressing 65,536 individual memory locations, the I/O address bus might be only eight lines wide, which means that 256 different I/O devices may be addressed.

Instruction Sets and Programming

The instructions of a microprocessor, you will recall, identify the individual operations that can be performed as single entities by logic within the microprocessor. There are five types of events that may be specified by individual instructions; they may be illustrated as follows:

Microprocessor Instructions

(1) Transferring data between the microprocessor and logic beyond the microprocessor

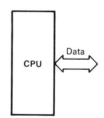

(2) Moving data from one register to another within the microprocessor

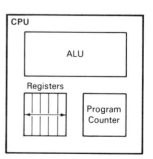

③ Specifying an arithmetic or
logic unit operation

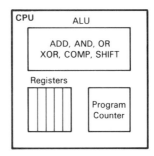

④ Modifying Program Counter (PC)
contents and thus enabling
programmed logic

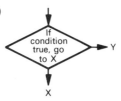

⑤ Status flag manipulation "condition" in
type **4** instruction is one example of status.

Let us consider these instruction types one at a time.

I/O Instructions **Instructions that move data between the microprocessor and external logic beyond the microprocessor may access memory or physical devices.** Physical devices beyond the microcomputer system are referred to generally as input/output (or I/O) devices. Instructions that access I/O devices are called I/O instructions. **Some microprocessors have separate instructions to transfer data between the microprocessor and I/O devices or memory.**

Microprocessor Instructions

① Transferring data between the
microprocessor and logic
beyond the microprocessor

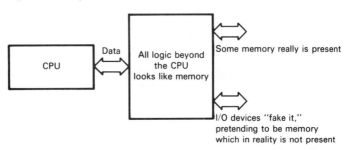

② Moving data from one register
to another within
the microprocessor

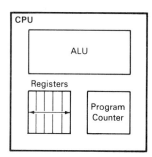

③ Specifying an arithmetic or
logic unit operation

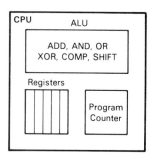

④ Modifying Program Counter (PC)
contents and thus enabling
programmed logic

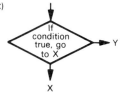

⑤ Status flag manipulation "condition" in
type **4** instruction is one example of status.

Other microprocessors use the same instructions to transfer data between the microprocessor and memory or I/O devices.

Microprocessor Instructions

① Transferring data between the microprocessor and logic beyond the microprocessor

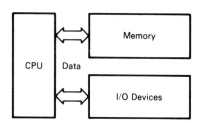

② Moving data from one register to another within the microprocessor

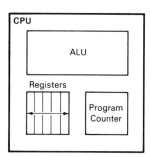

③ Specifying an arithmetic or logic unit operation

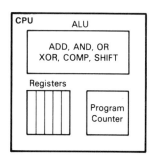

④ Modifying Program Counter (PC) contents and thus enabling programmed logic

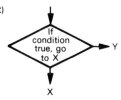

⑤ Status flag manipulation "condition" in type **4** instruction is one example of status.

You will recall from our earlier discussion of signals and buses that **there is really very little difference between I/O and memory reference instructions.** I/O reference instructions generate control signals identifying transfer of data to or from an I/O device.

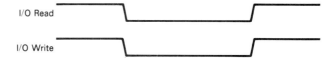

Memory Reference Instructions

Memory reference instructions generate equivalent signals.

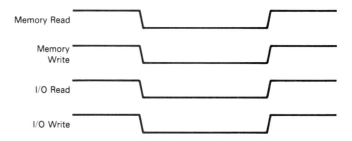

A microprocessor that uses the same instructions to access memory or an I/O device will simply have one set of control signals.

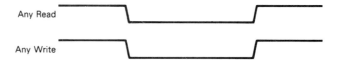

When a microprocessor uses the same control signals to access memory or I/O devices, logic associated with the memory address distinguishes between memory and an I/O device. Whoever designs the microcomputer decides which addresses will access memory, and which addresses will instead select an I/O device.

Note that just because a microprocessor has separate memory and I/O instructions, a microcomputer designer does not have to use the I/O instructions. The microcomputer designer could still address I/O devices as though they were memory locations. The converse is not true. A microprocessor that has no I/O instructions forces the microcomputer designer to address I/O devices as memory locations. In every case, you the microcomputer user have no choice. You must use memory reference and I/O reference instructions exactly as the microcomputer designer tells you to.

The number and complexity of instructions that move data between CPU registers is strictly a function of the number of registers provided by the microprocessor. Obviously, a microprocessor that only has one addressable register is not going to have any instructions to move data between registers. A microprocessor that has two addressable registers could have two such instructions.

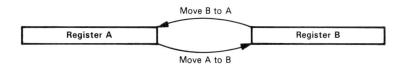

As the number of registers within the CPU increases, the microprocessor will run out of possibilities. Suppose, for example, a microprocessor has 16 addressable registers. In order to move data from any one of the 16 registers (as the source) to any one of the 16 registers (as the destination), the microprocessor instruction code must have some bits to identify every possible source register and destination register.

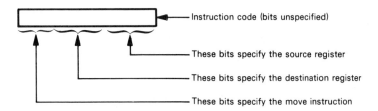

But it takes four instruction object code bits to identify one of 16 registers.

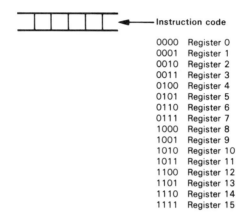

0000	Register 0
0001	Register 1
0010	Register 2
0011	Register 3
0100	Register 4
0101	Register 5
0110	Register 6
0111	Register 7
1000	Register 8
1001	Register 9
1010	Register 10
1011	Register 11
1100	Register 12
1101	Register 13
1110	Register 14
1111	Register 15

If four instruction object code bits are needed to specify the source register, and another four instruction object code bits are needed to specify the destination register, then for an 8-bit microprocessor, all eight instruction object code bits will be used up in specifying instructions that move data between a source register and a destination register.

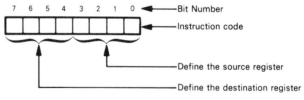

No codes left

Accumulator   One solution adopted by many microprocessor designers is to have a "primary" register, often referred to as an *accumulator*. The accumulator must be the source or the destination for any data movement within the CPU. Now instructions that move data from one location to another within a CPU must always move the data through the accumulator. For the case of 16 registers we now need just four bits to define the selected register.

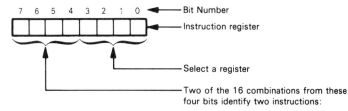

Notice that we can still move data from any one register to any other, but this operation is going to require two instructions rather than one. This may be illustrated as follows:

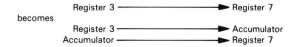

Let us now look at instructions that specify Arithmetic and Logic Unit operations. Generally, there are two classes of arithmetic and logic operations: those that require two operands and those that require one operand. The ADD, AND, OR, and Exclusive-OR operations require two operands.

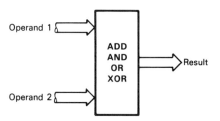

Complement, Shift, and Rotate operations require one operand.

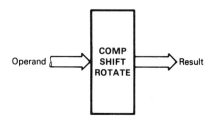

Operands can come from one of the following three locations:

· From a register within the microprocessor

· From an external memory or I/O location

· As a constant provided by the instruction itself.

Consider first two-operand instructions. You have six possibilities, just for the operands. Using the notation ( ) to signify "contents of," these possibilities may be illustrated as follows:

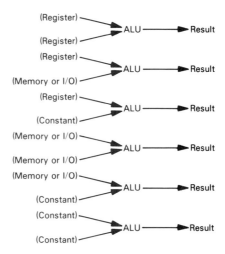

Let us arbitrarily select the ADD operation and examine the possibilities.

You might add the contents of one register to another. The sum may be stored in one of the two operand registers, in a third register, or in an external memory or I/O device location. Storing the result in a "constant" would be meaningless, since it would destroy the constant.

You could add the contents of a register and an external memory or I/O location. Once again, the sum could be stored in one of the operand locations, or in some separate location.

An instruction could also specify that the contents of two external memory or I/O locations be added, with the sum being stored in a register, in one of the operand locations, or in a different external memory or I/O location.

In practice, very few microprocessors have instructions that allow two operands to be fetched from two external memory locations. This is because the microprocessor must execute an external memory read for each operand, and that results in relatively complex overall instructions. For example, it would take four memory references, occurring within one instruction execution, in order to add the contents of two external memory locations. This may be illustrated as follows:

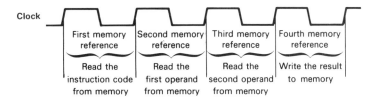

There is nothing intrinsically impossible about having a complex instruction, as illustrated above. In fact, many minicomputers have such instructions. But microprocessors are generally simpler than minicomputers. Typically, microprocessors are limited to the instruction fetch and one additional memory reference during one instruction's execution time. Therefore, one operand can come from memory (or an I/O device), or the result can be stored in memory or an I/O device, but not both.

An operand may also be a constant. The constant is provided by the instruction code. An instruction could, for example, specify that a constant value 3 be added to the contents of a CPU register or external memory location. An instruction that specifies a constant actually includes the constant as part of the instruction. This may be illustrated as follows:

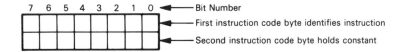

In reality a constant is nothing more than the contents of a location in program memory. But since program memory frequently becomes Read-Only Memory, the constant does indeed become a constant — because it resides in a part of memory that can never be modified.

Operations of the ALU that require a single operand may specify the contents of a register, memory location, or I/O device as the operand. Microprocessor instructions will not allow you to specify a constant as the input for a single-operand ALU instruction because that would make no sense. For example, an instruction to complement 3 would be an unnecessary instruction; you know what the complement of 3 is, so you might as well store this value in the first place. **Instructions that modify the program counter contents fall into one of the following three categories:**

· Instructions that unconditionally modify the program counter contents

· Instructions that modify the program counter contents only when specific conditions identified by appropriate status are met

· Instructions that save the contents of the program counter before modifying it. These instructions give you the opportunity to return to the point where the program counter contents were changed. You can return to the point where the program counter contents were changed by restoring to the program counter the value which you saved before changing it.

While instructions that move data and manipulate ALU logic are self-evident, instructions that manipulate the program counter contents are logically elusive to a novice programmer. This is because these instructions, along with status instructions, implement programming logic — a subject that will make no sense to you until you understand programming. We therefore defer until *Volume 1* any reasonable discussion of these instruction types.

The purpose of the foregoing summary of instruction types has been to identify the types of operations that may constitute a microprocessor's instruction set. Clearly, at this point you are a long way from looking at a microprocessor instruction set and being able to use it. You are, however, ready to move on to *An Introduction to Microcomputers: Volume 1 — Basic Concepts,* which covers essentially the same material as Chapters 4, 5, and 6 of this book, but in much more detail. By the time you have finished reading *Volume 1 — Basic Concepts,* you will be in a position to start using microprocessors.

A
How Information Is Stored

It would be possible to record information on the surface of a floppy disk, much as music is recorded on the surface of a record, in one continuous groove or one continuous track, spiraling out from the center of the floppy disk surface.

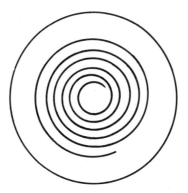

The problem with this kind of recording is that it would be very hard to pick your way around the recorded information. You can prove this for yourself by trying to find a particular word in a song on a record. If you struggle long enough, you will probably accomplish the task; but you will do so only by using your human judgment. Electronics cannot use human judgment, but can only follow set rules.

Thus, we will not use the single continuous spiraling track to record information. We will replace it with a large number of concentric tracks.

We can now select one particular track by its track number, which we can address by its exact distance from the edge or center of the floppy disk.

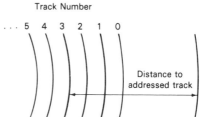

Different manufacturers use different numbers of tracks on each floppy disk surface. The only standard that exists is for eight-inch floppy disks, which frequently have 77 concentric tracks, numbered 0 through 76, recorded on one surface. Some floppy disks store information on one side of the disk only, while others store information on both sides.

You can store up to 1 million characters of information on one side of an eight-inch floppy disk. But if you were to simply divide up this information on the basis of track number, you would have some problems. First, tracks increase in length as they move from the center of the surface toward the circumference; this means that no two tracks would store the same amount of information. Secondly, the amount of information stored on one track could be quite large, yet it would represent the smallest single unit of addressable information on the surface of a floppy disk. If you address the surface of the floppy disk via track numbers only, then you must read the information off an entire track, or you must write information to an entire track.

Sectors

We can resolve these two problems by *sectoring* each track, that is, by storing the same amount of information on each track, no matter how close the track is to the center or circumference of the floppy disk surface. But this wastes more of the track as you move from the center toward the circumference of the floppy disk. Now you can identify information on the surface of the floppy disk by its track number and by the number of the sector within the track. Floppy disks commonly contain 26 sectors. If 128 characters of information are stored within each sector of each track, you calculate the total storage capacity of a single floppy disk surface as follows:

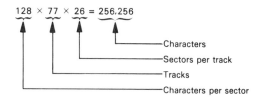

$$128 \times 77 \times 26 = 256,256$$

- Characters
- Sectors per track
- Tracks
- Characters per sector

Double Density Floppy Disk

Some manufacturers store 256 characters of information on each sector of a track; these are called *double density* floppy disks. Double density floppy disks use the same sector size as regular floppy disks, but they squeeze more information into the same space. These strange numbers of characters per sector, 128 or 256, are powers of 2 in the sequence 1, 2, 4, 8, 16, 32, 64, 128, 256, etc.

Hard Sectored Disk

Floppy disks have one or more holes punched in the surface of the disk to help the drive mechanism detect sectors. Some floppy disks have a hole punched between each sector; these are referred to as *hard sectored disks,* and may be illustrated as follows:

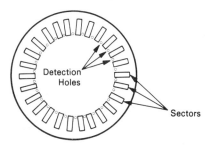

Detection Holes

Sectors

Soft Sectored Disk

Soft sectored disks have one punched hole only. This may be illustrated as follows:

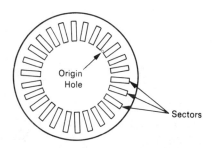

Origin Hole

Sectors

Floppy Disk
Formatting

When you buy a blank floppy disk its surface is completely blank. You cannot yet write onto the floppy disk. **Before writing onto a blank disk you must do a preliminary step called *formatting*. During the formatting step the floppy disk drive designates sectors and tracks using appropriate magnetic codes. This is an automatic process which you accomplish simply by following instructions; however, you must be aware of the need for this step.** Once you have formatted a blank floppy disk it is ready to be used. You can write information onto a formatted floppy disk and read the written information back.

Sector Chaining

Being able to go directly to any sector on the surface of a disk has another, less obvious advantage. What if you have a block of information that is too large to fit in a single sector? Suppose, for example, your block of information is so big that it must be stored on five sectors.

You could use a microcomputer system to create form letters. You could store 50 standard paragraphs on a floppy disk, then create a variety of letters by simply stringing selected paragraphs together. That is how most junk mail form letters are created. Each paragraph could become a unit of information which, in our example, is stored on five floppy disk sectors. Your immediate reaction may be to use five contiguous sectors.

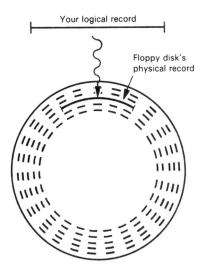

But since you can access sectors randomly, it makes no difference whether the five sectors are contiguous, as illustrated, or whether they are scattered randomly across the surface of the floppy disk.

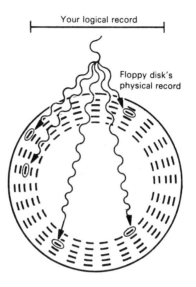

Chained Sectors   When you store a single unit of information on more than one sector, the sectors are said to be *chained*.

How Information is Stored on Cassettes

Information is stored on cassette tape as a sequence of physical records. There is no standard cassette format as there is with the sectors and tracks we described for a floppy disk. The physical records on a cassette tape may all have the same length or they may have various lengths; also, there are no restrictions placed on physical record length. A physical record may be one character long, or it may be as long as the length of the cassette tape will allow. The logical record we described when discussing floppy disk sectors and tracks can be recorded on cassette tape as a single physical record,

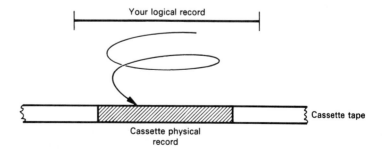

or it may be spread over a number of physical records.

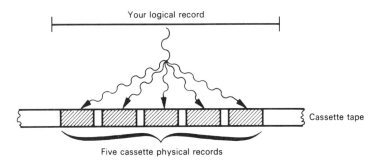

Cassette Inter-Record Gap   If you have more than one record on a cassette tape, then there must be inter-record gaps separating individual records. This may be illustrated as follows:

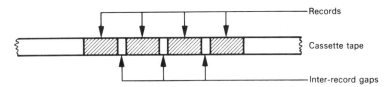

There is no useful information stored in an inter-record gap. As we increase the number of records on a cassette tape we increase the number of inter-record gaps, and we decrease the total amount of useful information that we can store on the cassette tape. **To get the most information on a cassette tape we should store the information as one continuous record** with no inter-record gaps.

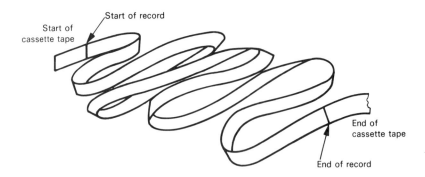

At the other extreme, if you have numerous very short records, you will waste most of the cassette tape on inter-record gaps.

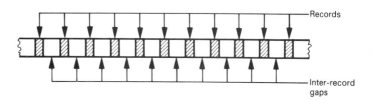

Cassette Tape Reliability

Redundant Recording

So why does anyone bother storing many short records? The answer is to fight errors. Cassettes are not very reliable; it is easy to scratch or damage the cassette tape surface, and the magnetic coating on the tape wears off as you use the cassette. **In order to help eliminate errors, well-designed microcomputer systems record every piece of information twice on a cassette tape. This is referred to as *redundant recording*.** Suppose you have just one long record per cassette tape; this will become two records if you use redundant recording. This may be illustrated as follows:

You can have one or more errors in one of the two records and still read the record correctly:

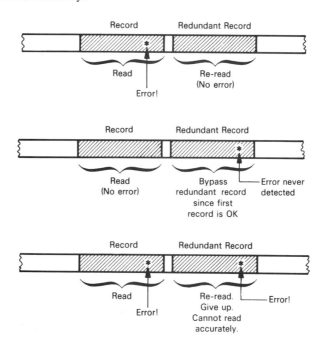

Now, suppose we break up the one long record into four shorter records. Each of the four shorter records will have its own redundant record, which means that there will be eight records on the cassette tape. This may be illustrated as follows:

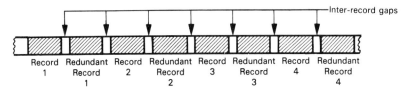

The two errors which would otherwise render the cassette tape unusable can now be tolerated. Remember, errors on a cassette tape will occur because the cassette tape is physically damaged. Thus, the two errors will reoccur in exactly the same physical locations on the cassette tape. This may be illustrated as follows:

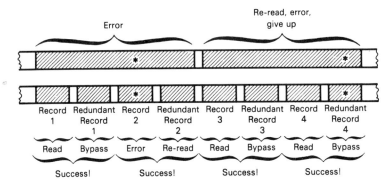

Our cassette tape is now more tolerant of errors, simply because we have increased the number of records.

We can now handle two additional errors before having to throw out the cassette tape. This may be illustrated as follows:

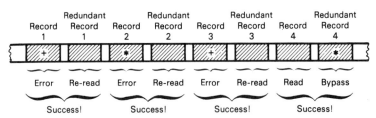

In summary, as the number of records on a cassette tape increases, the total amount of information you can record decreases, but your

**Error
Detection
Codes**

tolerance of errors goes up — provided you use redundant recording.
    A microcomputer system ensures that it has read a record correctly
by writing a special error detection code on the end of every record.
This special code is calculated by applying a formula to all of the
numbers in the record. This may be illustrated as follows:

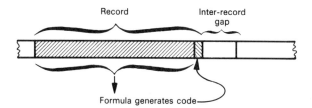

When the microcomputer system reads back a record, it calculates a
new error detection code, this time based on the numbers it reads back.
Then it reads back the old error detection code. If the record has been
read back correctly, the new and old error detection codes will be identical:

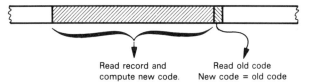

If any numbers have been read back incorrectly, then the new code
will not be the same as the old code; the information is therefore
assumed to be incorrect.

B
ASCII Character Codes

b4	b3	b2	b1	Row	0	1	2	3	4	5	6	7
			b7 →		0	0	0	0	1	1	1	1
			b6 →		0	0	1	1	0	0	1	1
			b5 →	Column	0	1	0	1	0	1	0	1
0	0	0	0	0	NUL	DLE	SP	0	@	P	`	p
0	0	0	1	1	SOH	DC1	!	1	A	Q	a	q
0	0	1	0	2	STX	DC2	''	2	B	R	b	r
0	0	1	1	3	ETX	DC3	#	3	C	S	c	s
0	1	0	0	4	EOT	DC4	$	4	D	T	d	t
0	1	0	1	5	ENQ	NAK	%	5	E	U	e	u
0	1	1	0	6	ACK	SYN	&	6	F	V	f	v
0	1	1	1	7	BEL	ETB	'	7	G	W	g	w
1	0	0	0	8	BS	CAN	(	8	H	X	h	x
1	0	0	1	9	HT	EM	)	9	I	Y	i	y
1	0	1	0	10	LF	SUB	*	:	J	Z	j	z
1	0	1	1	11	VT	ESC	+	;	K	[	k	{
1	1	0	0	12	FF	FS	,	<	L	\	l	|
1	1	0	1	13	CR	GS	-	=	M	]	m	}
1	1	1	0	14	SO	RS	.	>	N	^	n	~
1	1	1	1	15	SI	US	/	?	O	_	o	DEL

NUL	Null		DC1	Device control 1
SOH	Start of heading		DC2	Device control 2
STX	Start of text		DC3	Device control 3
ETX	End of text		DC4	Device control 4
EOT	End of transmission		NAK	Negative acknowledge
ENQ	Enquiry		SYN	Synchronous idle
ACK	Acknowledge		ETB	End of transmission block
BEL	Bell, or alarm		CAN	Cancel
BS	Backspace		EM	End of medium
HT	Horizontal tabulation		SUB	Substitute
LF	Line feed		ESC	Escape
VT	Vertical tabulation		FS	File separator
FF	Form feed		GS	Group separator
CR	Carriage return		RS	Record separator
SO	Shift out		US	Unit separator
SI	Shift in		SP	Space
DLE	Data link escape		DEL	Delete

C
Standard
Flowchart Symbols

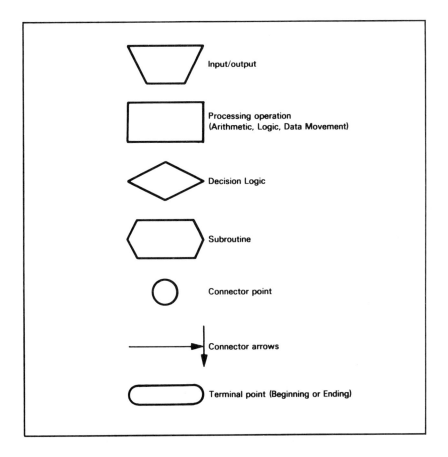

Flowcharts are a pictorial representation of computer program organization. They show the sequence of operations and are therefore helpful to the programmer in locating errors in program design. Flowcharts use the above standard symbols which are comprehensible to a non-programmer. The symbols used represent operations, data, flow, and equipment.

Index

About the Authors

Dr. Adam Osborne, President and General Manager of OSBORNE/ McGraw-Hill, has worked to produce a growing library of microcomputer books and software. He authored the well-known four volume series, *An Introduction to Microcomputers*, and co-authored titles in the *Programming for Logic Design* series. In 1979 Dr. Osborne explained the microcomputer revolution to the layman in *Running Wild — The Next Industrial Revolution*. He has contributed to many other books, including *Z8000 Assembly Language Programming, PET*^{TM}*/CBM*^{TM} *Personal Computer Guide*, and *CBASIC*^{TM} *User Guide*. In 1980 he founded Osborne Computer Corporation, manufacturer of the Osborne 1 personal computer.

He is an international speaker and has contributed numerous articles to journals in the microcomputer industry. Dr. Osborne received his B.S. degree from the University of Birmingham, England, and his Ph.D. in Chemical Engineering from the University of Delaware. He is currently working on his first novel.

Dave Bunnell is a pioneer in the microcomputer industry. He was Vice President of MITS, Inc. when they made the first microcomputer, the Altair 8800. He was the founding publisher of *Personal Computing* magazine, and has written many books and articles on the microcomputer industry. Mr. Bunnell is currently publisher of *PC: The Independent Guide to IBM Personal Computers*.

Other OSBORNE/McGraw-Hill Publications